DEPRESSION GLASS

& MORE

1920s – 1960s

IDENTIFICATION AND VALUES

TWELFTH EDITION
by
Gene Florence

COLLECTOR BOOKS
A Division of Schroeder Publishing Co., Inc.

Notice

The current values in this book should be used only as a guide. They are not intended to set prices, which vary from one section of the country to another. Auction prices as well as dealer prices vary greatly and are affected by condition as well as demand. Neither the author nor the publisher assumes responsibility for any losses that might be incurred as a result of consulting this guide.

A listing of the colors to be found in each pattern is mentioned under the photo headings. However, the prices cataloged herein represent those colors most commonly collected in each pattern. See *The Collector's Encyclopedia of Depression Glass* should you desire more detailed information.

On the cover:

Beaded Edge pattern, luncheon plate, $12.00; cup and saucer, $16.00; 5" bowl, $16.00; tumbler, $16.00.

Cover Design by Beth Summers
Layout Design By Holly C. Long

Searching For A Publisher?

We are always looking for knowledgeable people considered to be experts within their fields. If you feel that there is a real need for a book on your collectible subject and have a large comprehensive collection, contact Collector Books.

Collector Books
P.O. Box 3009
Paducah, KY 42002 – 3009

Gene Florence
P.O. Box 22185   P.O. Box 64
Lexington, KY 40522   Astatula, FL 34705

www.collectorbooks.com

Printed in USA.

Preface

Depression glass as defined in this book is the colored glassware made primarily during the Depression years in the colors of amber, green, pink, blue, red, yellow, white, and crystal. There are other colors and some of the glassware included in this book was made later than the Depression era; but it has still been collected as that glassware because of its color. The main emphasis of this book is given to the inexpensively made glassware produced in quantity and sold through the five and dime stores or given away as premiums or included with the purchase of other products, i.e., spice shakers containing a certain brand spice.

Information for this book has come from over 1,900,000 miles of travel throughout the country in connection with glassware over the past 29 years and from the research and sale of over 900,000 copies of *The Collector's Encyclopedia of Depression Glass.*

Acknowledgments

I would like at this time to say a word of thanks to the people who generously sent information and measurements to update listings in this book.

Also, a special thanks to my family for their support in various ways, gathering bits of information, taking over my household duties to leave me free to write.

Photography for this book was shared by Richard Walker and Charles R. Lynch. I wish to also thank the editorial staff of Collector Books for their work with the photography sessions and putting this book together.

Pricing

Glass that is in less than mint condition, i.e., chipped, cracked, scratched, or poorly molded, will bring very small prices unless extremely rare; and even then, will bring only a tiny percentage of the price of glass that is in mint condition.

This book is meant as a guide to price; however, if your Depression glass comes to you at bargain rates or free from a relative, then that's all to the good!

Prices have become almost standarized due to national advertising by dealers and due to the Depression glass shows which are held from coast to coast. However, there are some regional differences in prices due to glass being more readily available in some areas of the country than in others. Too, companies distributed certain pieces in some areas that they did not in others.

Contents

Contents

How to Find Depression Glass

The best place to find Depression glass is in your own basement, garage, or attic, or even in your own cupboards. Yes, that's true! Nearly everyone has at least a piece or two around their own home; it may be a bowl that belonged to grandmother and got handed down; it may be a complete setting that an aunt or someone got as a wedding gift and packed away for storage in the attic.

First of all, you need to learn to recognize the colors of Depression glass, for often the coloring of the glass is recognizable as Depression era glassware even when the pattern name is yet unknown. That was primarily the reason for making this a full-color book, so that the novice collector could acquaint himself with the full range of colors in which the glass may be found.

Once you have searched your own shelves and those of your immediate relatives and friends, your next source for finding Depression glass should be the garage sales, tag sales, yard sales, etc. where people are cleaning out their attics and garages. Don't forget the church bazaar, the Salvation Army store, or the Volunteers of America. You'll find competition is keen at these latter places; so, you'll need to shop early.

Now that you've covered all the aforementioned places, it's time to make a tour of the antique and junk shops in your area. These are often gold mines of the ridiculous to the sublime price-wise; have in mind what you'll pay for a particular item. Too, most of these shops expect to haggle a bit over price; don't be shy.

Household and estate auctions are often another valuable source for finding Depression glass, but it is wise to check out the merchandise before making a bid since chips and small damage to an item may be overlooked by the harried auctioneer.

Many collectors feel that antique shows and flea markets are the very best places to find Depression glass. Don't forget to put these on your agenda.

I find my best sources for finding particular pieces and patterns in Depression glass are the Depression glass shows held by clubs throughout the country and through the *Daze,* a publication which deals primarily in Depression era glass. You will find a listing on page 191 of this book. There are other publications, of course, but for overall information and volume of advertised glass, the *Daze* is it! Don't forget to check the Internet if you have access to that. Find me at www.geneflorence.com.

Selling Depression Glass

One of the purposes of this book is to help you make money from any of your unwanted glassware. Any number of books imply that there are treasures in your attic, but few tell you how to reap benefits from them. Finding a reputable dealer in your area is not always an easy task, but here are a few suggestions. If you live in an area where a show is held regularly, watch for advertisements and attend the show. You might find a buyer for your glass among the dealers at the show. If there is a Depression glass club meeting in your area, there may be members there who would be willing to buy your glass or who could put you in contact with someone who would. Failing either of those methods, you could send for a sample copy of one of the publications listed at the end of the book and seek a dealer in your area by looking through the ads. The telephone directory or the ads under "Antiques" in your local newspaper may lead you to a dealer in glass who would be interested in buying yours; or you might take it to a local flea market and find a buyer among the dealers set up there.

The prices herein are retail and you can expect to receive 50 to 70% of the prices listed for the popular, highly collectible patterns, but only 35 to 50% of prices listed for the patterns that are not as avidly sought by collectors.

There are several factors a dealer will consider when offering for your piece: its condition, how popular this color is with potential buyers, whether or not the pattern is one numerous people collect, whether he has plenty in stock already, or whether he thinks he can make money on the piece before he's had to pack it up at 65 different shows throughout the country or dropped it and broken it. Popularity of a pattern and the demand for it are the two key factors in interesting a potential buyer of your glassware. This book should give you an accurate guide as to what to expect for your glass. You shouldn't be walking up to a dealer without the faintest idea of what your glass is worth; neither should you expect him to pay you retail price for the glass if you're sincerely wanting him to buy it.

What to Collect

Many beginning collectors make the mistake of trying to collect everything in sight. Unless you have a few oil wells on the side, you can soon find yourself out of funds doing this.

My first suggestion is to study this book. Most of you have looked at the pictures before even starting to read this; that's a start. You have a general idea of what's available. Decide on one or possibly two patterns you like. Once you see it close at hand, you may change your mind; but that's all right. Collectors do that for a variety of reasons. However, it's wise to settle on something specific to look for rather than to pick and choose at random.

If money is a problem, peruse the prices of the various patterns and choose one that is less expensive to collect. However, you should become familiar with the whole range of patterns and you should have a general idea of the range of prices on the more expensive pieces of the patterns because everyone, sooner or later, stumbles onto a piece of glass worth $50.00 that's priced at $5.00. Even if you don't care for the piece or the pattern, you should go ahead and buy it because you'll either be able to trade it for the pattern you want, or you can sell it and use the extra money to buy the glass you like.

In the early 1960s through the early 1970s, you could buy Depression glass by the box and crate loads at auctions for a song; thus, you could afford to collect several patterns at once. However, those days have come to an end; so it's better to have something definite in mind to collect.

If money is no problem, then by all means, choose one of the more expensive patterns to collect. Since there are usually more people wanting these patterns, the market value of your pattern will be stable at the least, and will probably increase as the years pass.

Some people don't choose to collect an entire pattern. They collect one piece of every pattern, maybe plates for example. One California collector collects only cookie jars; another I know collects only candy jars; and there are numerous salt and pepper collections. You could choose to collect only one or two pieces of several patterns. In any case, you'll find the glass attractive to serve in and a real item of conversation.

If you are hard-bitten by the bug of collecting Depression Glass, then you might possibly want a more detailed guide for the glass. Should that happen, I'd be delighted to recommend my *Collector's Encyclopedia of Depression Glass* or *Collectible Glassware of the '40s, '50s, & '60s,* which can be ordered from this publisher or myself. I receive letters daily from its delighted readers. In any case, happy hunting and finding. It's a hobby I think you'll not only enjoy but one from which you'll profit.

ADAM

(See Reproduction Section, Page 167)
(pink, green, crystal, yellow, delphite)
JEANNETTE GLASS COMPANY, 1932 – 1934

	Pink	Green		Pink	Green
Ashtray, 4½"	30.00	25.00	Plate, 6" Sherbet	11.00	12.00
Bowl, 4¾" Dessert	22.00	22.00	Plate, 7¾" Sq. Salad	18.00	18.00
Bowl, 5¾" Cereal	55.00	50.00	Plate, 9" Sq. Dinner	35.00	30.00
Bowl, 7¾"	30.00	30.00	Plate, 9" Grill	28.00	22.00
Bowl, 9" Covered	70.00	90.00	Platter, 11¾"	30.00	35.00
Bowl, 10" Oval	35.00	40.00	Relish Dish, 8" Divided	20.00	25.00
Butter Dish & Cover	110.00	395.00	Salt & Pepper, 4"	100.00	115.00
Cake Plate, 10" Footed	30.00	33.00	Saucer, Sq. 6"	6.00	6.00
Candlesticks, 4", Pr.	115.00	115.00	Sherbet, 3"	35.00	38.00
Candy Jar & Cover, 2½"	110.00	115.00	Sugar	20.00	20.00
Coaster, 3¾"	22.00	20.00	Sugar/Candy Cover	25.00	45.00
Creamer	25.00	25.00	Tumbler, 4½"	32.00	30.00
Cup	30.00	25.00	Tumbler, 5½" Iced Tea	65.00	65.00
Lamp	295.00	325.00	Vase, 7½"	395.00	90.00
Pitcher, 8", 32 oz.	45.00	45.00			

AMERICAN PIONEER
(pink, green, amber, crystal)
LIBERTY WORKS, 1931 – 1934

	Pink	Green
Bowl, 5" Handled	20.00	20.00
Bowl, 8¾" Covered	125.00	135.00
Bowl, 9" Handled	30.00	35.00
Bowl, Console, 10¾"	55.00	65.00
Candlesticks, 6½", Pr.	100.00	125.00
Candy Jar & Cover, 1 lb.	85.00	100.00
Candy Jar & Cover, 1½ lb.	100.00	135.00
Cheese & Cracker Set (indented platter & compote)	55.00	65.00
Coaster, 3½"	35.00	35.00
Creamer, 2¾"	25.00	20.00
Creamer, 3½"	20.00	22.00
Cup	10.00	12.00
Dresser Set (2 colognes, Powder jar, on indented 7½" tray)	425.00	400.00
Goblet, Wine, 4", 3 oz.	40.00	55.00
Goblet, Water, 6", 8 oz.	45.00	60.00
Ice Bucket, 6"	55.00	65.00

	Pink	Green
Lamp, 8½" Tall	100.00	110.00
Mayonnaise, 4¼"	60.00	90.00
Pitcher, 5" Covered Urn	175.00	225.00
Pitcher, 7" Covered Urn	195.00	250.00
Plate, 6"	12.50	15.00
Plate, 6" Handled	12.50	15.00
Plate, 8"	13.00	15.00
Plate, 11½" Handled	30.00	35.00
Saucer	4.00	5.00
Sherbet, 3½"	16.00	20.00
Sherbet, 4¾"	35.00	40.00
Sugar, 2¾"	20.00	22.00
Sugar, 3½"	20.00	22.00
Tumbler, 5 oz. Juice	35.00	40.00
Tumbler, 4", 8 oz.	30.00	50.00
Tumbler, 5", 12 oz.	45.00	55.00
Vase, 7", four styles, rolled or crimped edge, straight	100.00	125.00
Whiskey, 2¼", 2 oz.	50.00	90.00

AMERICAN SWEETHEART ⊂━━━━━━━━━━━━⊃
(pink, monax, cremax, red and blue)
MacBETH-EVANS GLASS COMPANY, 1930 – 1936

	Pink	Monax		Pink	Monax
Bowl, 3¾" Flat, Berry	90.00	----	Plate, 15½"	----	250.00
Bowl, 4½" Cream Soup	95.00	120.00	Platter, 13" Oval	55.00	70.00
Bowl, 6" Cereal	18.00	18.00	Pitcher, 7½", 60 oz.	995.00	----
Bowl, 9" Round, Berry	50.00	70.00	Pitcher, 8", 80 oz.	750.00	----
Bowl, 9½" Flat Soup	75.00	90.00	Salt & Pepper, Footed	575.00	460.00
Bowl, 11" Oval Vegetable	70.00	80.00	Saucer	4.00	2.25
Bowl, 18" Console	----	495.00	Sherbet, Footed, 3¾"	25.00	----
Creamer, Footed	15.00	12.00	Sherbet, Footed, 4¼"	24.00	22.00
Cup	20.00	11.00	Sugar, Open, Footed	12.00	10.00
Plate, 6" Bread & Butter	6.00	6.50	Sugar Cover	----	495.00
Plate, 8" Salad	12.00	10.00	Tumbler, 3½", 5 oz	100.00	----
Plate, 9" Luncheon	----	14.00	Tumbler, 4¼", 9 oz.	90.00	----
Plate, 9¾"-10¼" Dinner	42.50	27.50	Tumbler, 4¾", 10 oz.	120.00	----
Plate, 12" Salver	25.00	25.00			

ANNIVERSARY

(pink) (late 1960s – mid 1970s in crystal and iridescent)
JEANNETTE GLASS COMPANY, 1947 – 1949

	Crystal	Pink		Crystal	Pink
Bowl, 4⅞" Berry	3.50	10.00	Plate, 9" Dinner	6.00	15.00
Bowl, 7⅜" Soup	9.00	17.50	Plate, 12½" Sandwich		
Bowl, 9" Fruit	14.00	30.00	Server	10.00	25.00
Butter Dish & Cover	27.50	60.00	Relish Dish, 8"	5.00	14.00
Candy Jar & Cover	28.00	50.00	Saucer	1.50	2.00
Cake Plate, 12½"	10.00	20.00	Sherbet, Footed	3.50	10.00
Cake Plate with Cover	18.00	----	Sugar	4.50	9.00
Compote, Open, 3 Legged	5.00	15.00	Sugar Cover	6.00	11.00
Creamer, Footed	5.00	12.00	Vase, 6½"	13.00	30.00
Cup	4.50	9.00	Vase, Wall Pin-up	20.00	35.00
Pickle Dish, 9"	5.00	15.00	Wine Glass, 2½ oz.	10.00	20.00
Plate, 6¼" Sherbet	2.00	4.00			

AUNT POLLY

(green, blue, iridescent)
U.S. GLASS COMPANY, Late 1920s

	Green	Blue		Green	Blue
Bowl, 4⅜" Berry	9.00	18.00	Creamer	30.00	55.00
Bowl, 4¾", 2" High	18.00	----	Pitcher, 8", 48 oz.	----	215.00
Bowl, 5½", One Handle	15.00	25.00	Plate, 6" Sherbet	6.00	15.00
Bowl, 7¼" Oval, Handled Pickle	15.00	40.00	Plate, 8" Luncheon	----	20.00
Bowl, 7⅞" Large Berry	20.00	45.00	Salt & Pepper	----	250.00
Bowl, 8⅜" Oval	55.00	135.00	Sherbet	10.00	12.00
Butter Dish & Cover	275.00	225.00	Sugar	25.00	30.00
Candy, Cover, Two Handled	75.00	----	Sugar Cover	60.00	165.00
Candy, Footed, Two Handled	25.00	50.00	Tumbler, 3⅝", 8 oz.	----	35.00
			Vase, 6½", Footed	35.00	55.00

AURORA

(cobalt, pink, green)
HAZEL ATLAS COMPANY, 1937 – 1938

	Cobalt		Cobalt
Bowl, 4½"	60.00	Plate, 6½"	13.00
Bowl, 5⅜"	18.00	Saucer	6.00
Creamer, 4½"	25.00	Tumbler, 4¾"	27.00
Cup	16.00		

AVOCADO, "SWEET PEAR," No. 601 ⊂━━━━━⊃
(See Reproduction Section, Page 168)
(pink, green, crystal, white)
INDIANA GLASS COMPANY, 1923 – 1933

	Pink	Green		Pink	Green
Bowl, 5¼", Two-Handled....	30.00	35.00	Pitcher, 64 oz.	900.00	1,500.00
Bowl, 6" Relish, Footed....	30.00	35.00	Plate, 6¾" Sherbet	20.00	20.00
Bowl, 7" Preserve, One			Plate, 8¼" Luncheon	18.00	22.00
Handle	30.00	35.00	Plate, 10½" Two Handled		
Bowl, 7½" Salad	50.00	70.00	Cake	45.00	65.00
Bowl, 8" Oval,			Saucer	22.50	24.00
Two-Handled................	30.00	35.00	Sherbet	55.00	65.00
Bowl, 9½", 3¼" Deep	140.00	195.00	Sugar, Footed	35.00	40.00
Creamer, Footed	35.00	40.00	Tumbler	195.00	300.00
Cup, Footed, ...	35.00	40.00			

BEADED BLOCK

(pink, green, crystal, ice blue, vaseline, iridescent, amber, opalescent colors)
IMPERIAL GLASS COMPANY, 1927 – 1930s

	Green	Opalescent
Bowl, 4½", Two-Handled Jelly	20.00	32.00
Bowl, 4½", Round, Lily	18.00	40.00
Bowl, 5½", Square	18.00	28.00
Bowl, 5½", One Handle	20.00	28.00
Bowl, 6", Deep, Round	25.00	35.00
Bowl, 6¼", Round	25.00	35.00
Bowl, 6½", Round	25.00	35.00
Bowl, 6½", Two-Handled Pickle	30.00	40.00
Bowl, 6¾", Round, Unflared	25.00	50.00
Bowl, 7¼", Round, Flared	30.00	38.00

	Green	Opalescent
Bowl, 7½", Round, Fluted Edges	30.00	45.00
Bowl, 7½", Round, Plain Edge	30.00	40.00
Bowl, 8¼", Celery	35.00	55.00
Creamer	25.00	40.00
Pitcher, 5¼", Pint Jug	110.00	----
Plate, 7¾" Square	18.00	30.00
Plate, 8¾", Round	20.00	35.00
Stemmed Jelly, 4½"	18.00	35.00
Stemmed Jelly, 4½", Flared Top	18.00	40.00
Sugar	25.00	40.00
Vase, 6", Bouquet	25.00	35.00

BEADED EDGE
(pattern #22 Milk Glass)
WESTMORELAND GLASS COMPANY, Late 1930s – 1950s

	Plain	Decorated		Plain	Decorated
Creamer, Ftd.	11.00	17.50	Platter, 12", Oval w/Tab		
Creamer, Ftd. w/Lid #108 .	20.00	32.00	Hndls.	40.00	100.00
Cup	5.00	12.00	Relish, 3 Part	50.00	----
Nappy, 5"	4.50	16.00	Salt and Pepper, Pr.	22.00	55.00
Nappy, 6", Crimped, Oval.	7.00	20.00	Saucer	2.00	4.00
Plate, 6", Bread & Butter.	5.00	9.00	Sherbet, Ftd.	6.50	15.00
Plate, 7", Salad	7.00	12.00	Sugar, Ftd.	12.50	17.50
Plate, 8½", Luncheon	7.00	12.00	Sugar, Ftd. w/Lid #108...	20.00	32.00
Plate, 10½", Dinner	12.00	40.00	Tumbler, 8 oz., Ftd.	8.00	18.00
Plate, 15", Torte	22.00	70.00			

BLOCK OPTIC, "BLOCK"
(green, yellow, pink, crystal)
HOCKING GLASS COMPANY, 1929 – 1933

	Pink	Green
Bowl, 4¼", Berry	12.00	9.00
Bowl, 5¼", Cereal	30.00	15.00
Bowl, 7¼", Salad	165.00	175.00
Bowl, 8½", Large Berry	35.00	30.00
Butter Dish & Cover, 3"x5"..	----	50.00
Candlesticks, 1¾", Pr.	80.00	120.00
Candy Jar & Cover, 2¼" Tall	60.00	60.00
Candy Jar Cover, 6¼" Tall	185.00	65.00
Compote, 4" Wide Mayonnaise	90.00	90.00
Creamer, Three Styles: Cone Shaped, Round Footed & Flat	14.00	13.00
Cup, Four Styles	7.00	7.00
Goblet, 4", Cocktail	40.00	40.00
Goblet, 4½", Wine	40.00	40.00
Goblet, 5¾", 9 oz.	36.00	27.00
Ice Bucket	75.00	45.00
Ice Tub or Butter Tub, Open..	100.00	65.00
Mug, Flat Creamer, No Spout	----	35.00
Pitcher, 7⅝", 54 oz.	135.00	80.00
Pitcher, 8½", 54 oz.	50.00	60.00
Pitcher, 8", 80 oz.	130.00	100.00
Plate, 6", Sherbet	3.00	3.00

	Pink	Green
Plate, 8", Luncheon	7.00	7.00
Plate, 9", Dinner	40.00	25.00
Salt & Pepper, Footed	90.00	45.00
Salt & Pepper, Squatty	----	125.00
Sandwich Server, Center Handle	75.00	75.00
Saucer, 2 Sizes, Cup Ring..	8.00	10.00
Sherbet, Non-Stemmed (Cone)	----	4.00
Sherbet, 3¼", 5½ oz.	7.50	6.00
Sherbet, 4¾", 6 oz.	18.00	18.00
Sugar, Three Styles: As Creamer	12.50	12.50
Tumbler, 3½", 5 oz., Flat	28.00	25.00
Tumbler, 3¼", 3 oz., Footed ..	30.00	30.00
Tumbler, 9½ oz., Flat	15.00	15.00
Tumbler, 9 oz., Footed	15.00	18.00
Tumbler, 10 oz., Flat	18.00	22.00
Tumbler, 6", 10 oz., Footed	35.00	35.00
Tumbler, 15 oz., Flat	40.00	45.00
Tumble-Up Night Set: 3" Tumbler Bottle & Tumbler, 6" High	----	70.00
Vase, 5¾", Blown	----	350.00
Whiskey, 2¼", 2 oz.	32.00	32.00

"BOWKNOT"
(green)
UNKNOWN MANUFACTURER

	Green		Green
Bowl, 4½", Berry	20.00	Sherbet, Low Footed	20.00
Bowl, 5½", Cereal	35.00	Tumbler, 5", 10 oz.	25.00
Cup	11.00	Tumbler, 5", 10 oz. Footed	25.00
Plate, 7", Salad	15.00		

"BUBBLE," "FIRE KING"
(blue, dark green, ruby red, crystal)
HOCKING GLASS COMPANY, 1934 – 1965

	Crystal	Blue
Bowl, 4", Berry	4.00	18.00
Bowl, 4½", Fruit	4.50	15.00
Bowl, 5¼", Cereal	10.00	14.00
Bowl, 7¾", Flat Soup	12.00	15.00
Bowl, 8⅜", Large Berry	10.00	17.00
Creamer	6.00	35.00
Cup	3.50	5.00
Pitcher, 64 oz., Ice Lip	100.00	60.00*
Plate, 6¾", Bread & Butter	3.00	3.00
Plate, 9⅜", Grill	----	22.50
Plate, 9⅜", Dinner	7.00	7.00

	Crystal	Blue
Platter, 12", Oval	15.00	16.00
Saucer	1.00	1.00
Sugar	6.00	25.00
Tumbler, 6 oz., Juice (Red)	3.50	8.00
Tumbler, 9 oz., Water (Red)	5.00	9.00
Tumbler, 12 oz., Iced Tea (Red)	12.00	12.50
Tumbler, 16 oz., Lemonade (Red)	14.00	16.00

* Red

CAMEO, "BALLERINA," or "DANCING GIRL"

(green, yellow, pink, and crystal with a platinum rim)
HOCKING GLASS COMPANY, 1930 – 1934

	Green	Yellow
Bowl, 4¾", Cream Soup	160.00	----
Bowl, 5½", Cereal	33.00	33.00
Bowl, 7¼", Salad	60.00	----
Bowl, 8¼", Large Berry....	45.00	----
Bowl, 9", Rimmed Soup	75.00	----
Bowl, 10", Oval Vegetable ..	35.00	42.00
Bowl, 11", Three-Leg Console......................	85.00	110.00
Butter Dish & Cover	235.00	1,500.00
Cake Plate, 10", Three Legs	25.00	----
Candlesticks, 4", Pr.	110.00	----
Candy Jar, Low 4" Cover..	90.00	110.00
Candy Jar, 6½" Tall & Cover	185.00	----
Cocktail Shaker (Metal Lid) Appears in Crystal Only..	----	900.00
Compote, 4" wide Mayonnaise................	40.00	----

	Green	Yellow
Cookie Jar & Cover........	55.00	----
Creamer, 3¼"	24.00	22.00
Creamer, 4¼"	28.00	----
Cup, Two Styles	15.00	7.50
Decanter, 10" w/Stopper ..	185.00	----
Decanter, 10" w/Stopper, Frosted (Stoppers Represent ½ value of Decanter)	40.00	----
Domino Tray, 7" w/3" Indentation	150.00	----
Goblet, 3½", Wine..........	1,000.00	----
Goblet, 4", Wine	80.00	----
Goblet, 6", Water	65.00	----
Ice Bowl or Open Butter 3" Tall x 5½" Wide	185.00	----
Jam Jar, 2" & Cover	185.00	----
Pitcher, 5¾", Syrup or Milk, 20 oz.	315.00	2,000.00

21

CAMEO, "BALLERINA," or "DANCING GIRL"

	Green	Yellow
Pitcher, 6", Juice, 36 oz...	65.00	----
Pitcher, 8½", Water, 56 oz.	60.00	----
Plate, 6", Sherbet	5.00	3.00
Plate, 8", Luncheon	12.00	11.00
Plate, 8½", Square	50.00	250.00
Plate, 9½", Dinner	22.00	10.00
Plate, 10", Sandwich	20.00	----
Plate, 10½", Grill	14.00	8.00
Plate, 10½", Grill w/Closed Handles	75.00	6.00
Plate, 10½" w/Closed Handles	12.00	12.00
Platter, 12" Closed Handles	25.00	45.00
Relish, 3-Part, 7½", Footed	35.00	----
Salt & Pepper, Footed, Pr.	70.00	----
Sandwich Server, Center Handle	7,000.00	----
Saucer w/Cup Ring	195.00	----

	Green	Yellow
Saucer, 6" (Sherbet Plate)..	5.00	3.00
Sherbet, 3⅛"	16.00	40.00
Sherbet, 4⅞"	35.00	45.00
Sugar, 3¼"	22.00	20.00
Sugar, 4¼"	30.00	----
Tumbler, 3¾", Juice, 5 oz.	33.00	----
Tumbler, 4", Water, 9 oz.	30.00	----
Tumbler, 4¾", Flat, 10 oz.	30.00	----
Tumbler, 5", Flat, 11 oz. ..	30.00	60.00
Tumbler, 5¼", 15 oz.	80.00	----
Tumbler, Footed Juice, 3 oz.	65.00	----
Tumbler, 5", Footed, 9 oz.	28.00	18.00
Tumbler, 5¾", Footed, 11 oz.	70.00	----
Vase, 5¾"	250.00	----
Vase, 8"	45.00	----
Water Bottle (Dark Green) Whitehouse Vinegar ..	25.00	----

CAPRI "SEASHELL," "SWIRL COLONIAL," "COLONIAL," "ALPINE"

HAZEL WARE, DIVISION OF CONTINENTAL CAN, 1960s

	Blue
Ashtray, 3¼", Triangular	6.00
Ashtray, 3¼", Round	6.00
Ashtray, 3½", Square, Embossed Flower	17.50
Ashtray, 5", Round	8.00
Ashtray, 6⅞", Triangular	12.00
Bowl, 4¾", Octagonal	7.50
Bowl, 4¾", Swirled	6.00
Bowl, 4⅞", Round, "Dots"	7.00
Bowl, 5⅜", Salad, Round, 'Hobnails"	8.00
Bowl, 5⅝", "Colony Swirl"	9.00
Bowl, 5¾", Square, Deep, Colony	10.00
Bowl, 6", Round, Tulip	12.00
Bowl, 6", Round, "Dots"	8.00
Bowl, 6", Round, Sq. Bottom, Colony	8.00
Bowl, 6¹⁄₁₆", Round, "Colony Swirl"	8.00
Bowl, 7¾", Oval, Colony	15.00
Bowl, 7¾", Rectangular, Colony	14.00
Bowl, 8¾", Swirled	12.00
Bowl, 9⅛" x 3" High	25.00
Bowl, 9½" x 2⅞" High	22.00
Bowl, 9½" oval 1½" High	9.00
Bowl, 10¾", Salad, Colony	26.00
Candy Jar, w/Cover, Ftd	32.00
Chip and Dip, 2 Swirled Bowls (8¾" and 4¾" on metal rack)	28.00
Creamer, Round	12.00
Cup, Octagonal	6.00
Cup, Round, "Hobnails"	5.00
Cup, Round, Swirled	5.00
Cup, Round, Tulip	8.00
Plate, 5¾", Bread and Butter, Octagonal	5.00
Plate, 7", Salad, Round, "Colony Swirl"	7.00
Plate, 7⅛", Round, Salad, "Colony Swirl"	7.00
Plate, 7¼", Salad, "Hobnails"	6.50
Plate, 7¼", Salad, Octagonal	7.50
Plate, 8", Square	9.00

	Blue
Plate, 8", Square, w/Square Cup Rest.	8.00
Plate, 8⅞", Square	10.00
Plate, 8⅞", Square, w/Round Cup Rest.	9.00
Plate, 9½", Round, Snack w/Cup Rest, Tulip	10.00
Plate, 9¾", Dinner, Octagonal	10.00
Plate, 9⅞", Dinner, Round, "Hobnails".	8.00
Plate, 10", Snack, Fan Shaped w/ Cup Rest	8.00
Saucer, 5½" Square	2.00
Saucer, 6", Round, "Hobnails"	1.50
Saucer, Octagonal	1.50
Stem, 4½", Sherbet	7.50
Stem, 5½", Water	9.00
Sugar w/Lid, Round	20.00
Tidbit, 3 Tier (Round 9⅞" Plate, 7⅛" Plate, 6" Saucer)	22.50
Tumbler, 2¾", 4 oz., "Colony Swirl"	7.00
Tumbler, 3", 4 oz., Fruit "Dots"	5.00
Tumbler, 3", 5 oz., Pentagonal Bottom	7.00
Tumbler, 3¹⁄₁₆", Colony or "Colony Swirl".	8.00
Tumbler, 3⅛", 5 oz., Pentagonal	8.00
Tumbler, 3¼", 8 oz., Old Fashioned, "Dots"	7.50
Tumbler, 3⅝", 3 oz., "Dots"	5.00
Tumbler, 4", "Dots"	7.00
Tumbler, 4¼", 9 oz., "Colony Swirl"	7.50
Tumbler, 4¼", 9 oz., Water, Pentagonal Bottom	7.50
Tumbler, 5", 12 oz., "Colony Swirl".	10.00
Tumbler, 5", 12 oz., Tea, Pentagonal Bottom	10.00
Tumbler, 5¼", "Dots"	6.00
Tumbler, 5½", 12 oz., Tea, Swirl	10.00
Tumbler, 6", 10 oz., "Dots"	8.00
Vase, 8", "Dots"	20.00
Vase, 8½", Ruffled	35.00

CHERRYBERRY

(pink, green, iridescent)
U.S. GLASS COMPANY, 1928 – 1931

	Pink or Green		Pink or Green
Bowl, 4", Berry	14.00	Pickle Dish	22.00
Bowl, 6¼", 2" Deep	125.00	Pitcher, 7¾"	185.00
Bowl, 6½" Deep, Salad	25.00	Plate, 6", Sherbet	12.00
Bowl, 7½" Deep, Berry	28.00	Plate, 7½", Salad	20.00
Butter Dish & Cover	185.00	Sherbet	11.00
Compote, 5¾"	28.00	Sugar, Small, Open	23.00
Creamer, Small	23.00	Sugar, Large	30.00
Creamer, Large, 4⅝"	42.50	Sugar Cover	65.00
Olive Dish, 5", One Handle	22.00	Tumbler, 3⅝", 9 oz.	38.00

CHERRY BLOSSOM

(See Reproduction Section, Pages 169 – 172) (pink, green, delphite, crystal)
JEANNETTE GLASS COMPANY, 1930 – 1939

	Pink	Green
Bowl, 4¾", Berry	20.00	19.00
Bowl, 5¾", Cereal	55.00	50.00
Bowl, 7¾", Flat Soup	95.00	90.00
Bowl, 8½", Round Berry	50.00	50.00
Bowl, 9", Oval Vegetable	50.00	45.00
Bowl, 9", Two-Handled	50.00	75.00
Bowl, 10½", 3-Leg Fruit	100.00	100.00
Butter Dish & Cover	50.00	110.00
Cake Plate (3 Legs) 10¼"	32.00	38.00
Coaster	14.00	14.00
Creamer	23.00	22.00
Cup	23.00	23.00
Mug, 7 oz.	295.00	225.00
Pitcher, 6¾" AOP, 36 oz. Scalloped or Round Bottom	65.00	60.00
Pitcher, 8" PAT, 36 oz. Ftd.	60.00	60.00
Pitcher, 8" PAT, 42 oz. Flat	60.00	60.00
Plate, 6", Sherbet	8.00	10.00
Plate, 7", Salad	25.00	24.00
Plate, 9", Dinner	26.00	27.00
Plate, 9", Grill	32.00	32.00
Platter, 9", Oval	1,000.00	1,100.00
Platter, 11", Oval	55.00	55.00
Platter, 13" & 13" Divided	70.00	70.00
Salt & Pepper Scalloped Bottom	1,300.00	1,100.00

	Pink	Green
Saucer	5.00	5.00
Sherbet	20.00	22.00
Sugar	15.00	18.00
Sugar Cover	20.00	20.00
Tray, 10½", Sandwich, Two Handled	30.00	33.00
Tumbler, 3¾", 4 oz., Footed AOP, Round	20.00	22.00
Tumbler, 4½", 9 oz., Round Foot AOP	40.00	40.00
Tumbler, 4½", 8 oz., Scalloped Foot AOP	40.00	40.00
Tumbler, 3½", 4 oz., Flat PAT	22.00	33.00
Tumbler, 4¼", 9 oz., Flat PAT	18.00	26.00
Tumbler, 5", 12 oz., Flat PAT	70.00	85.00

CHILD'S JUNIOR DINNER SET

	Pink
Creamer	50.00
Sugar	50.00
Original box	35.00
Plate, 6"	12.50
Cup	40.00
Saucer	7.50
14-piece Set	340.00

CHINEX CLASSIC
(ivory, ivory decorated)
MacBETH-EVANS DIVISION OF CORNING GLASS WORKS
Late 1930s – Early 1940s

	Ivory	Decorated		Ivory	Decorated
Bowl, 5¾", Cereal	5.50	9.00	Plate, 6¼", Sherbet	2.50	3.50
Bowl, 6¾", Salad	12.00	20.00	Plate, 9¾", Dinner	4.50	9.00
Bowl, 7", Vegetable	15.00	25.00	Plate, 11½", Sandwich		
Bowl, 7¾", Flat Soup	12.50	22.00	or Cake	7.50	14.00
Bowl, 9", Vegetable	12.00	25.00	Saucer	2.00	4.00
Butter Dish	55.00	75.00	Sherbet, Low Footed	7.00	11.00
Creamer	6.00	10.00	Sugar, Open	6.00	10.00
Cup	4.50	6.50			

CHRISTMAS CANDY
(crystal, teal)
INDIANA GLASS COMPANY, 1950s

	Crystal	Teal		Crystal	Teal
Bowl, 5¾", Fruit	4.50	----	Plate, 8¼", Luncheon	7.00	30.00
Bowl, 7⅜", Soup	7.00	50.00	Plate, 9⅝", Dinner	10.00	48.00
Bowl, 9½", Vegetable	----	550.00	Plate, 11¼", Sandwich	15.00	65.00
Creamer	9.00	33.00	Saucer	2.00	12.00
Cup	5.00	33.00	Sugar	9.00	33.00
Plate, 6", Bread & Butter	3.50	12.50			

CIRCLE

(green, pink, crystal)
HOCKING GLASS COMPANY, 1930s

	Green or Pink		Green or Pink
Bowl, 4½".................................	8.00	Plate, 8¼", Luncheon	4.00
Bowl, 5", Flared	16.00	Plate, 10", Sandwich	14.00
Bowl, 8"	18.00	Saucer	1.50
Bowl, 9⅜".................................	25.00	Sherbet, 3⅛"	4.00
Creamer	10.00	Sherbet, 4¾"	6.00
Cup	5.00	Sugar	10.00
Goblet, 4½", Wine	12.50	Tumbler, 4 oz., Juice	8.00
Goblet, 8 oz., Water.....................	11.00	Tumbler, 8 oz., Water	9.00
Pitcher, 60 oz.	75.00	Tumbler, 10 oz.	18.00
Pitcher, 80 oz.	35.00	Tumbler, 15 oz.	25.00
Plate, 6", Sherbet........................	2.00		

CLOVERLEAF
(pink, green, yellow, black)
HAZEL ATLAS GLASS COMPANY, 1930 – 1936

	Green	Yellow
Ashtray, 4", Match Holder in Center (black only)	65.00	----
Ashtray, 5¾", Match Holder in Center (black only)	90.00	----
Bowl, 4", Dessert	35.00	35.00
Bowl, 5", Cereal	50.00	50.00
Bowl, 7", Salad	55.00	65.00
Bowl, 8"	80.00	----
Candy Dish & Cover	55.00	115.00
Creamer, Footed, 3⅝"	10.00	20.00
Cup	9.00	11.00

	Green	Yellow
Plate, 6", Sherbet	8.00	10.00
Plate, 8", Luncheon	8.00	14.00
Plate, 10¼", Grill	25.00	28.00
Salt & Pepper, Pr.	40.00	125.00
Saucer	3.00	4.00
Sherbet, 3" Footed	12.00	14.00
Sugar, Footed, 3⅝"	10.00	20.00
Tumbler, 3¾", 9 oz., Flat	60.00	----
Tumbler, 4", 10 oz., Flat	45.00	----
Tumbler, 5¾", 10 oz., Footed	28.00	38.00

COIN GLASS
(amber, blue, crystal, green, olive, red)
LINE #1372, FOSTORIA GLASS COMPANY, 1958 – 1982

	Blue	Crystal
Ashtray, 5" #1372/123	25.00	18.00
Ashtray, 7½", Center Coin #1372/119	----	25.00
Ashtray, 7½", Round #1372/114	40.00	25.00
Ashtray, 10" #1372/124	50.00	25.00
Ashtray, Oblong #1372/115	20.00	10.00
Ashtray/Cover, 3" #1372/110	25.00	25.00
Bowl, 8", Round #1372/179	50.00	25.00
Bowl, 8½", Ftd. #1372/199	90.00	50.00
Bowl, 8½", Ftd. w/Cover #1372/212	175.00	90.00
*Bowl, 9", Oval #1372/189	55.00	30.00
*Bowl, Wedding w/Cover #1372/162	90.00	55.00
Candle Holder, 4½", Pr. #1372/316	50.00	40.00
Candle Holder, 8", Pr. #1372/326	----	50.00
Candy Box w/Cover, 4⅛" #1372/354	60.00	30.00
*Candy Jar w/Cover, 6⁵⁄₁₆" #1372/347	50.00	25.00
*Cigarette Box w/Cover, 5¾" x 4½" #1372/374	80.00	40.00
Cigarette Holder w/Ashtray Cover #1372/372	75.00	45.00

* Items recently remade.

30

COIN GLASS

	Blue	Crystal
Cigarette Urn, 3⅜", Ftd. #1372/381	45.00	20.00
Condiment Set, 4 Pc. (Tray, 2 Shakers and Cruet) #1372/737..	325.00	135.00
Condiment Tray, 9⅝", #1372/738	75.00	40.00
*Creamer #1372/680	16.00	10.00
Cruet, 7 oz. w/Stopper #1372/531	165.00	55.00
*Decanter w/Stopper, Pint, 10³⁄₁₆" #1372/400	250.00	95.00
*Jelly #1372/448	25.00	15.00
Lamp Chimney, Coach or Patio #1372/461	60.00	40.00
Lamp Chimney, Hndl., Courting #1372/292	65.00	----
Lamp, 9¾", Hndl., Courting, Oil #1372/310	170.00	----
Lamp, 10⅛", Hndl., Courting, Electric #1372/311	200.00	----
Lamp, 13½", Coach, Electric #1372/321	225.00	95.00
Lamp, 13½", Coach, Oil #1372/320	225.00	95.00
Lamp, 16⅝", Patio, Electric #1372/466	275.00	135.00
Lamp, 16⅝", Patio, Oil #1372/459	275.00	135.00
Nappy, 4½" #1372/495	----	25.00
*Nappy, 5⅜", w/Hndl. #1372/499	30.00	15.00
Pitcher, 32 oz., 6⁵⁄₁₆" #1372/453	135.00	55.00
Plate, 8", #1372/550	----	20.00
Punch Bowl Base #1372/602	----	165.00
Punch Bowl, 14", 1½ gal., #1372/600	----	165.00
Punch Cup #1372/615	----	32.00
*Salver, Ftd., 6½" Tall #1372/630	225.00	125.00
Shaker, 3¼", Pr. w/Chrome Top #1372/652	65.00	25.00
Stem, 4", 5 oz. Wine #1372/26	----	35.00
Stem, 5¼", 9 oz., Sherbet, #1372/7	----	25.00
Stem, 10½ oz., Goblet #1372/2	----	40.00
*Sugar w/Cover #1372/673	45.00	25.00
Tumbler, 3⅝", 9 oz. Juice/Old Fashioned #1372/81	----	30.00
Tumbler, 4¼", 9 oz. Water, Scotch & Soda #1372/73	----	30.00
Tumbler, 5⅛", 12 oz. Iced Tea/High Ball #1372/64	----	38.00
Tumbler, 5⅜", 10 oz. Double Old Fashioned #1372/23	----	30.00
Tumbler, 5⁵⁄₁₆", 14 oz. Iced Tea #1372/58	----	38.00
*Urn, 12¾", Ftd., w/Cover #1372/829	125.00	75.00
Vase, 8", Bud #1372/799	40.00	20.00
Vase, 10", Ftd. #1372/818	----	45.00

* Items recently remade.

COLONIAL, "KNIFE AND FORK"
(pink, green, crystal)
HOCKING GLASS COMPANY, 1934 – 1938

	Pink	Green
Bowl, 3¾"	53.00	----
Bowl, 4½", Berry	18.00	20.00
Bowl, 5½", Cereal	65.00	100.00
Bowl, 4½", Cream Soup	75.00	75.00
Bowl, 7", Low Soup	65.00	65.00
Bowl, 9", Large Berry	35.00	35.00
Bowl, 10", Oval Vegetable	40.00	40.00
Butter Dish & Cover	700.00	55.00
Creamer, 5", 16 oz., (Milk Pitcher)	65.00	25.00
Cup	12.00	14.00
Goblet, 3¾", 1 oz., Cordial	----	30.00
Goblet, 4", 3 oz., Cocktail	----	25.00
Goblet, 4½", 2½ oz., Wine	----	28.00
Goblet, 5¼", 4 oz., Claret	----	25.00
Goblet, 5¾", 8½ oz., Water	----	33.00
Mug, 4½", 12 oz.	500.00	800.00
Pitcher, 7", 54 oz., Ice Lip or None	70.00	55.00
Pitcher, 7¾", 68 oz., Ice Lip or None	70.00	80.00
Plate, 6", Sherbet	6.00	9.00

	Pink	Green
Plate, 8½", Luncheon	10.00	11.00
Plate, 10", Dinner	55.00	65.00
Plate, 10", Grill	25.00	25.00
Platter, 12", Oval	35.00	25.00
Salt & Pepper, Pr.	140.00	150.00
Saucer (Same as sherbet plate)	6.00	9.00
Sherbet	12.00	15.00
Spoon Holder or Celery	135.00	130.00
Sugar, 5"	25.00	15.00
Sugar Cover	65.00	25.00
Tumbler, 3", 5 oz., Juice	22.00	25.00
Tumbler, 4", 9 oz., Water	22.00	22.00
Tumbler, 11 oz.	35.00	42.00
Tumbler, 12 oz., Iced Tea	52.00	52.00
Tumbler, 15 oz., Lemonade	65.00	75.00
Tumbler, 3¼", 3 oz., Footed	18.00	25.00
Tumbler, 4", 5 oz., Footed	32.00	42.00
Tumbler, 5¼", 10 oz., Footed	50.00	50.00
Whiskey, 2½", 1½ oz	15.00	16.00

COLONIAL BLOCK

(green, pink, crystal, white)
HAZEL ATLAS GLASS COMPANY, Late 1920s – Early 1930s

	Green or Pink		Green or Pink
Bowl, 4"	8.00	Goblet	12.50
Bowl, 7"	22.00	Pitcher	45.00
Butter Dish	45.00	Sherbet	8.00
Butter Tub	45.00	Sugar	10.00
Candy Dish & Cover, 8½"	40.00	Sugar Cover	12.00
Creamer	12.00	Tumbler, 5¼", 5 oz. ftd	55.00

COLONIAL FLUTED, "ROPE"
(green, crystal)
FEDERAL GLASS COMPANY, 1928 – 1933

	Green		Green
Bowl, 4", Berry	11.00	Plate, 6", Sherbet	3.00
Bowl, 6", Cereal	15.00	Plate, 8", Luncheon	7.00
Bowl, 6½", Deep Salad	35.00	Saucer	2.00
Bowl, 7½", Large Berry	22.00	Sherbet	7.00
Creamer	10.00	Sugar	10.00
Cup	8.00	Sugar Cover	16.00

COLUMBIA
(crystal, pink)
FEDERAL GLASS COMPANY, 1938 – 1942

	Crystal	Pink		Crystal	Pink
Bowl, 5", Cereal	18.00	----	Plate, 9½", Luncheon	10.00	35.00
Bowl, 8", Low Soup	22.00	----	Plate, 11", Chop	15.00	----
Bowl, 8½", Salad	20.00	----	Saucer	2.00	10.00
Bowl, 10½", Ruffled Edge ..	20.00	----	Snack Plate	30.00	----
Butter Dish & Cover	20.00	----	Tumbler, 4 oz.	25.00	----
Cup	8.50	25.00	Tumbler, 9 oz.	35.00	----
Plate, 6", Bread & Butter	3.50	15.00			

CORONATION, "BANDED FINE RIB," "SAXON"

(pink, crystal, green, Royal Ruby)
HOCKING GLASS COMPANY, 1936 – 1940

	Pink	Red		Pink	Red
Bowl, 4¼", Berry	7.00	7.00	Plate, 8½", Luncheon	5.00	----
Bowl, 6½", Nappy	6.00	18.00	Saucer	3.00	----
Bowl, 8", Large Berry	15.00	18.00	Sherbet	8.00	----
Cup	7.50	6.50	Tumbler, 5", 10 oz.,		
Pitcher, 7¾", 68 oz.	550.00	----	Footed	33.00	----
Plate, 6", Sherbet	3.00	----			

CREMAX

(cremax, decal decorations)
MacBETH-EVANS DIVISION OF CORNING GLASS WORKS
Late 1930s – Early 1940s

	Ivory	Ivory Decorated		Ivory	Ivory Decorated
Bowl, 5¾", Cereal	3.50	10.00	Plate, 9¾", Dinner	4.50	12.00
Bowl, 9", Vegetable	8.00	20.00	Plate, 11½", Sandwich	5.50	20.00
Creamer	4.50	10.00	Saucer	2.00	3.50
Cup	4.00	5.00	Saucer, Demitasse	5.00	----
Cup, Demitasse	15.00	----	Sugar, Open	4.50	10.00
Plate, 6¼", Bread & Butter	2.00	4.00			

CROCHETED CRYSTAL
IMPERIAL GLASS COMPANY, 1943 – Early 1950s

	Crystal		Crystal
Basket, 6"	30.00	Mayonnaise Bowl, 5¼"	12.50
Basket, 9"	40.00	Mayonnaise Ladle	5.00
Basket, 12"	70.00	Mayonnaise Plate, 7½"	7.50
Bowl, 7", Narcissus	40.00	Plate, 8", Salad	7.50
Bowl, 10½", Salad	30.00	Plate, 9½"	12.50
Bowl, 11", Console	30.00	Plate, 13", Salad Bowl Liner	22.50
Bowl, 12", Console	32.50	Plate, 14"	25.00
Buffet Set, 14" Plate, Ftd., Sauce Bowl, Ladle	45.00	Plate, 17"	40.00
Cake Stand, 12", ftd.	40.00	Punch Bowl, 14"	65.00
Candleholder, 4½", 2-Lite	15.00	Punch Cup Closed Hdld.	5.00
Candleholder (Narcissus Bowl Shape)	33.00	Punch Cup, Open Hdld.	8.00
Celery, 10", Oval	25.00	Relish, 11½", 3 pt.	25.00
Cheese & Cracker, 12" Plate, Ftd. Dish	40.00	Stem, 4½", 3½ oz., Cocktail	12.50
		Stem, 5½", 4½ oz., Wine	17.50
		Stem, 5", 6 oz., Sherbet	10.00
Creamer	20.00	Stem, 7⅛", 9 oz., Water Goblet	14.00
Epergne, 11", Ftd. Bowl, Center Vase.	130.00	Sugar	20.00
Hors d'oeuvre Dish, 10½", 4 pt., Round	30.00	Tumbler, 6", 6 oz., Ftd. Fruit Juice	10.00
Lamp, 11", Hurricane w/Shade	50.00	Tumbler, 7⅛", 12 oz., Ftd. Iced Tea	15.00
		Vase, 8"	35.00

"CROW'S FOOT"

(Ritz blue, Ruby red, amber, amethyst, black, pink, crystal, white, and yellow)
PADEN CITY GLASS COMPANY, LINE 412 & LINE 890, 1930s

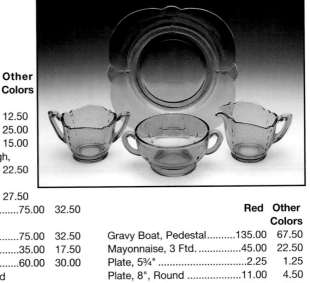

	Red	Other Colors
Bowl, 4⅞", Square	25.00	12.50
Bowl, 8¾" Sq.	50.00	25.00
Bowl, 6"	40.00	15.00
Bowl, 6½", Rd., 2½" High, 3½" Base	45.00	22.50
Bowl, 8½", Square, 2-Hdld.	60.00	27.50
Bowl, 10", Ftd.	75.00	32.50
Bowl, 10", Sq, 2-Hdld	75.00	32.50
Bowl, 11", Oval	35.00	17.50
Bowl, 11", Square	60.00	30.00
Bowl, 11", Square, Rolled Edge	65.00	32.50
Bowl, 11½", 3 Ftd.,Round Console	85.00	42.50
Bowl, 11½", Console	75.00	37.50
Bowl, Cream Soup, Ftd./Flat	22.00	10.00
Bowl, Nasturtium, 3 Ftd.	185.00	95.00
Bowl, Whipped Cream, 3 Ftd.	55.00	27.50
Cake Plate, Sq., Low Pedestal	85.00	42.50
Candle, Round Base, Tall	75.00	37.50
Candle, Square, Mushroom	37.50	20.00
Candlestick, 5¾"	25.00	12.50
Candy w/Cover, 6½", 3 Part 2 Styles)	75.00	50.00
Candy, 3 Ftd., Rd., 6⅛" Wide, 3¼" High	150.00	80.00
Cheese Stand, 5"	25.00	12.50
Comport, 3¼" Tall, 6¼" Wide	27.50	15.00
Comport 4¾" Tall, 7⅜" Wide	50.00	35.00
Comport, 6⅝" Tall, 7" Wide	75.00	30.00
Creamer, Flat	12.50	6.50
Creamer, Ftd.	12.50	6.50
Cup, Ftd. or Flat	10.00	5.00
Gravy Boat, Flat	85.00	40.00

	Red	Other Colors
Gravy Boat, Pedestal	135.00	67.50
Mayonnaise, 3 Ftd.	45.00	22.50
Plate, 5¾"	2.25	1.25
Plate, 8", Round	11.00	4.50
Plate, 8½", Square	12.00	3.50
Plate, 9¼", Round, Small Dinner	35.00	15.00
Plate, 9½", Rd., 2-Hdld.	65.00	32.50
Plate, 10⅜", Rd., 2-Hdld.	50.00	25.00
Plate, 10⅜", Sq., 2-Hdld.	40.00	20.00
Plate, 10½", Dinner	90.00	40.00
Plate, 11", Cracker	45.00	22.50
Platter, 12"	50.00	15.00
Relish, 11", 3 pt.	85.00	45.00
Sandwich Server, Rd., Center Handled	65.00	32.50
Sandwich Server, Sq., Center Handled	45.00	17.50
Saucer, 6", Round	2.50	1.00
Saucer, 6", Square	3.00	1.50
Sugar, Flat	11.00	5.50
Sugar, Ftd.	11.00	5.50
Tumbler, 4¼"	75.00	37.50
Vase, 4⅝" Tall, 4⅛" Wide	70.00	40.00
Vase, 10¼", Cupped	100.00	45.00
Vase, 10¼", Flared	95.00	32.50
Vase, 11¾", Flared	150.00	65.00

CUBE, "CUBIST"
(pink, green, crystal)
JEANNETTE GLASS COMPANY, 1929 – 1933

	Pink	Green		Pink	Green
Bowl, 4½", Dessert	6.50	7.00	Plate, 8", Luncheon	10.00	11.00
Bowl, 4½" Deep	8.00	----	Powder Jar & Cover,		
Bowl, 6½", Salad	10.00	15.00	Three Legs	30.00	33.00
Butter Dish & Cover	70.00	65.00	Salt & Pepper, Pr.	35.00	35.00
Candy Jar & Cover, 6½"	30.00	33.00	Saucer	2.50	2.50
Coaster, 3¼"	9.00	9.00	Sherbet, Footed	10.00	11.00
Creamer, 2⅝"	2.00	----	Sugar, 2"	2.00	----
Creamer, 3³⁄₁₆"	10.00	12.00	Sugar, 3"	7.00	8.00
Cup	7.50	9.00	Sugar/Candy Cover	15.00	15.00
Pitcher, 8¾", 45 oz.	210.00	235.00	Tumbler, 4", 9 oz.	72.00	78.00
Plate, 6" Sherbet	3.50	4.00			

"CUPID"

(amber, blue, black, pink, green)
PADEN CITY GLASS COMPANY, 1930s

	Green/Pink		Green/Pink
Bowl, 8½" Oval-Ftd.	275.00	Creamer, 5" Ftd.	150.00
Bowl, 9¼" Ftd. Fruit	295.00	Ice Bucket, 6"	325.00
Bowl, 9¼" Center-Handled	275.00	Ice Tub, 4¾"	325.00
Bowl, 10¼", Fruit	215.00	Mayonnaise, 6" Diameter, Fits on 8"	
Bowl, 10½", Rolled Edge	200.00	Plate, Spoon, 3-Pc.	195.00
Bowl, 11" Console	200.00	Plate, 10½"	150.00
Cake Plate, 11¾"	215.00	Samovar	995.00
Cake Stand, 2" High, Ftd.	215.00	Sugar, 4¼" Ftd.	150.00
Candlestick, 5" Wide, Pr.	245.00	Sugar, 5" Ftd.	150.00
Candy w/Lid, Ftd., 5¼" High	395.00	Tray, 10¾" Center-Handled	215.00
Candy w/Lid, 3 Part	295.00	Tray, 10⅞" Oval-Ftd.	250.00
Casserole, Covered	495.00	Vase, 8¼" Elliptical	650.00
Comport, 6¼"	195.00	Vase, Fan-Shaped	450.00
Creamer, 4½" Ftd.	150.00	Vase, 10"	325.00

"DAISY," NUMBER 620

(crystal, 1933; amber, 1940; dark green and milk glass, 1960s)
INDIANA GLASS COMPANY

	Crystal	Amber		Crystal	Amber
Bowl, 4½", Berry	4.50	9.00	Plate, 9⅜", Dinner	5.50	9.00
Bowl, 4½", Cream Soup	4.50	12.00	Plate, 10⅜", Grill	5.50	10.00
Bowl, 6", Cereal	10.00	33.00	Plate, 11½", Cake or		
Bowl, 7⅜", Berry	7.50	15.00	Sandwich	7.00	15.00
Bowl, 9⅜", Deep Berry	13.00	35.00	Platter, 10¾"	7.50	18.00
Bowl, 10", Oval Vegetable	10.00	18.00	Relish Dish, 3 Part, 8⅜"	13.00	35.00
Creamer, Footed	6.00	8.00	Saucer	1.50	2.00
Cup	4.00	6.00	Sherbet, Footed	5.00	9.00
Plate, 6", Sherbet	2.00	3.00	Sugar, Footed	6.00	8.00
Plate, 7⅜", Salad	3.50	7.00	Tumbler, 9 oz., Footed	10.00	20.00
Plate, 8⅜", Luncheon	4.00	6.00	Tumbler, 12 oz., Footed	20.00	40.00

DELLA ROBBIA
(crystal decorated, opaque blue, white)
#1058 WESTMORELAND GLASS COMPANY, Late 1920s – 1940s

	Crystal w/trim		Crystal w/trim
Basket, 9"	195.00	Plate, 6⅛", Bread & Butter	10.00
Basket, 12"	295.00	Plate, 7¼", Salad	22.00
Bowl, 4½", Nappy	27.50	Plate, 9", Luncheon	35.00
Bowl, 5", Finger	35.00	Plate, 10½", Dinner	145.00
Bowl, 6", Nappy, Bell	40.00	Plate, 14", Torte	115.00
Bowl, 6½", One Hdld. Nappy	35.00	Plate, 18"	200.00
Bowl, 7½", Nappy	45.00	Plate, 18", Upturned Edge, Punch	
Bowl, 8", Bell Nappy	55.00	Bowl Liner	200.00
Bowl, 8", Bell, Hdld.	75.00	Platter, 14", Oval	175.00
Bowl, 8", Heart, Hdld.	165.00	Punch Bowl Set, 15 pc	895.00
Bowl, 9", Nappy	95.00	Salt and Pepper, Pr.	65.00
Bowl, 12", Ftd.	135.00	Salver, 14", Ftd., Cake	155.00
Bowl, 13", Rolled Edge	135.00	Saucer	10.00
Bowl, 14", Oval, Flange	250.00	Stem, 3 oz., Wine	28.00
Bowl, 14", Punch	300.00	Stem, 3¼ oz., Cocktail	25.00
Bowl, 15", Bell	225.00	Stem, 5 oz., 4¾", Sherbet, High Foot.	25.00
Candle, 4"	40.00	Stem, 5 oz., Sherbet, Low Foot ..	22.00
Candle, 4", 2-Lite	125.00	Stem, 6 oz., Champagne	25.00
Candy Jar w/Cover, Scalloped Edge .	100.00	Stem, 8 oz., 6", Water	35.00
Candy, Round, Flat, Chocolate ...	95.00	Sugar, Ftd.	18.00
Comport, 6½", 3⅝" High, Mint, Ftd.	30.00	Tumbler, 5 oz., Ginger Ale	25.00
Comport, 8", Sweetmeat, Bell	110.00	Tumbler, 8 oz., Ftd.	30.00
Comport, 12", Ftd., Bell	125.00	Tumbler, 8 oz., Water	25.00
Comport, 13", Flanged	125.00	Tumbler 11 oz., Iced Tea, Ftd.	35.00
Creamer, Ftd.	18.00	Tumbler 12 oz., Iced Tea, Bell	38.00
Cup, Coffee	18.00	Tumbler 12 oz., Iced Tea, Bell, Ftd.	38.00
Cup, Punch	15.00	Tumbler 12 oz., 5³⁄₁₆", Iced Tea,	
Pitcher, 32 oz.	250.00	Straight	40.00
Plate, 6", Finger Liner	12.00		

DEWDROP

(crystal, iridescent)
JEANNETTE GLASS COMPANY, 1953 – 1956

	Crystal		Crystal
Bowl, 4¾"	5.00	Plate, Snack, w/Indent For Cup	5.00
Bowl, 8½"	12.00	Punch Bowl Base	10.00
Bowl, 10⅜"	17.50	Punch Bowl, 6 qt.	30.00
Butter, w/Cover	27.50	Relish, Leaf Shape w/Hndl	8.00
Candy dish, w/Cover, 7", Round	22.00	Sugar, w/Cover	13.00
Creamer	8.00	Tray, 13", Lazy Susan	45.00
Cup, Punch or Snack	4.00	Tumbler, 9 oz., Water	16.00
Pitcher, ½ Gallon	22.00	Tumbler, 15 oz., Iced Tea	20.00
Plate, 11½"	17.50		

DIAMOND QUILTED, "FLAT DIAMOND"
(pink, blue, green, crystal, black)
IMPERIAL GLASS COMPANY, Late 1920s – Early 1930s

	Green	Blue
Bowl, 4¾", Cream Soup	10.00	20.00
Bowl, 5", Cereal..................	7.50	15.00
Bowl, 5½", One Handle	7.50	22.00
Bowl, 7", Crimped Edge	9.00	22.00
Bowl, Rolled Edge Console	20.00	60.00
Cake Salver, Tall, 10" Diameter	60.00	----
Candlesticks (2 styles), Pr.	25.00	50.00
Candy Jar & Cover, Footed	65.00	----
Compote & Cover, 11½"	95.00	----
Creamer...........................	12.00	20.00
Cup	9.50	17.50
Goblet, 1 oz. Cordial	12.00	----
Goblet, 2 oz. Wine	12.00	----
Goblet, 3 oz, Wine	12.00	----
Goblet, 6", 9 oz., Champagne....................	11.00	----
Ice Bucket	55.00	85.00

	Green	Blue
Mayonnaise Set: Ladle, Plate, Three-Footed Dish	38.00	60.00
Pitcher, 64 oz.	50.00	----
Plate, 6", Sherbet...............	4.00	7.00
Plate, 7", Salad	6.00	11.00
Plate, 8", Luncheon	6.00	14.00
Plate, 14", Sandwich	15.00	----
Punch Bowl & Stand	495.00	----
Sandwich Server, Center Handle	25.00	50.00
Saucer	4.00	7.00
Sherbet	9.00	16.00
Sugar	12.00	20.00
Tumbler, 9 oz., Water	9.00	----
Tumbler, 12 oz., Iced Tea ..	9.00	----
Tumbler, 6 oz., Footed	8.50	----
Tumbler, 9 oz., Footed	12.50	----
Tumbler, 12 oz., Footed	15.00	----
Whiskey, 1½ oz..................	8.00	----

DIANA
(pink, amber, crystal)
FEDERAL GLASS COMPANY, 1937 – 1941

	Pink	Amber		Pink	Amber
Ashtray, 3½"	3.50	----	Plate, 6", Bread & Butter	5.00	2.00
Bowl, 5", Cereal	10.00	14.00	Plate, 9½", Dinner	20.00	9.00
Bowl, 5½", Cream Soup	25.00	20.00	Plate, 11¾", Sandwich	25.00	10.00
Bowl, 9", Salad	22.00	18.00	Platter, 12", Oval	33.00	15.00
Bowl, 11", Console Fruit	45.00	18.00	Salt & Pepper, Pr.	85.00	110.00
Bowl, 12", Scalloped Edge.	30.00	20.00	Saucer	5.00	2.00
Candy Jar & Cover, Round.	50.00	40.00	Sherbet	12.00	10.00
Coaster, 3½"	8.00	10.00	Sugar, Open, Oval	12.00	8.00
Creamer, Oval	12.00	9.00	Tumbler, 4⅛", 9 oz.	50.00	30.00
Cup	20.00	9.00			
Cup, Demitasse, 2 oz. & 4½" Saucer Set	45.00	----			

DOGWOOD, "APPLE BLOSSOM," "WILD ROSE"

(pink, green, crystal, yellow)
MacBETH EVANS COMPANY, 1929 – 1932

	Pink	Green
Bowl, 5½", Cereal	35.00	35.00
Bowl, 8½", Berry	65.00	125.00
Bowl, 10¼", Fruit	550.00	295.00
Cake Plate, 11", Heavy Solid Foot	1,200.00	----
Cake Plate, 13", Heavy Solid Foot	145.00	135.00
Coaster, 3¼"	550.00	----
Creamer, 2½", Thin	20.00	48.00
Creamer, 3¼", Thick	25.00	----
Cup, Thin or Thick	18.00	40.00
Pitcher, 8", 80 oz., Decorated	250.00	525.00
Pitcher, 8", 80 oz., (American Sweetheart Style)	650.00	----
Plate, 6", Bread & Butter.	9.00	11.00
Plate, 8", Luncheon	7.00	9.00

	Pink	Green
Plate, 9¼", Dinner	40.00	----
Plate, 10½", Grill AOP or Border Design Only	25.00	25.00
Plate, 12", Salver	35.00	----
Platter, 12", Oval (Rare)	750.00	----
Saucer	6.00	8.00
Sherbet, Low Footed	38.00	115.00
Sugar, 2½", Thin	18.00	45.00
Sugar, 3¼", Thick	16.00	----
Tumbler, 3½", 5 oz., Decorated	250.00	----
Tumbler, 4", 10 oz., Decorated	42.00	98.00
Tumbler, 4¾", 11 oz., Decorated	48.00	100.00
Tumbler, 5", 12 oz., Decorated	68.00	120.00
Tumbler, Moulded band	22.00	----

DORIC

(pink, green, Delphite, yellow)
JEANNETTE GLASS COMPANY, 1935 – 1938

	Pink	Green
Bowl, 4½", Berry	11.00	11.00
Bowl, 5", 2 Handled Cream Soup	----	450.00
Bowl, 5½", Cereal	75.00	85.00
Bowl, 8¼", Large Berry	30.00	32.00
Bowl, 9", Two Handled	20.00	25.00
Bowl, 9", Oval Vegetable	40.00	45.00
Butter Dish & Cover	70.00	85.00
Cake Plate, 10", 3 Legs	27.00	30.00
Candy Dish & Cover, 8"	40.00	42.00
Candy Dish, Three Part	12.00	10.00
Coaster, 3"	18.00	18.00
Creamer, 4"	16.00	14.00
Cup	10.00	12.00
Pitcher, 6", 36 oz., Flat	40.00	45.00
Pitcher, 7½", 48 oz., Ftd.	700.00	1,150.00
Plate, 6", Sherbet	6.00	7.00
Plate, 7", Salad	20.00	25.00
Plate, 9", Dinner	18.00	19.00
Plate, 9", Grill	22.00	25.00
Platter, 12", Oval	30.00	35.00
Relish Tray, 4" x 4"	15.00	10.00
Relish Tray, 4" x 8"	22.00	18.00
Salt & Pepper, Pr.	35.00	37.50
Saucer	3.50	4.50
Sherbet, Footed	15.00	17.00
Sugar	12.00	12.50
Sugar Cover	20.00	30.00
Tray, 10", Handled	20.00	20.00
Tray, 8" x 8", Serving	25.00	30.00
Tumbler, 4½", 9 oz., Flat	75.00	110.00
Tumbler, 4", 10 oz., Ftd.	65.00	90.00
Tumbler, 5", 12 oz., Ftd.	80.00	125.00

DORIC AND PANSY
(pink, crystal, ultramarine)
JEANNETTE GLASS COMPANY, 1937 – 1938

	Pink	Ultramarine
Bowl, 4½", Berry.........	12.00	22.00
Bowl, 8", Large Berry...	30.00	90.00
Bowl, 9", Handled........	20.00	40.00
Butter Dish & Cover.....	----	450.00
Cup.............................	----	16.00
Creamer.......................	----	115.00
Plate, 6", Sherbet........	8.00	11.00
Plate, 7", Salad............	----	40.00
Plate, 9", Dinner..........	----	40.00
Salt & Pepper, Pr.........	----	400.00
Saucer........................	----	5.00
Sugar, Open................	----	110.00
Tray, 10", Handled.......	----	35.00
Tumbler, 4½", 9 oz.......	----	120.00

"PRETTY POLLY PARTY DISHES"	Pink	Ultramarine
Cup..............................	35.00	45.00
Saucer.........................	7.00	8.00
Plate	8.00	11.00
Creamer.......................	35.00	50.00
Sugar...........................	35.00	50.00
14-Piece Set................	275.00	355.00

ENGLISH HOBNAIL
(crystal, pink, amber, turquoise, cobalt, green)
WESTMORELAND GLASS COMPANY, 1920s – 1970s

	Pink or Green
Ashtray, Several Shapes	20.00
Bowls, 4½", 5" Square & Round	20.00
Bowl, Cream Soup	25.00
Bowls, 6", Several Styles	18.00
Bowls, 8", Several Styles	45.00
Bowls, 8", Footed & Two-Handled.	85.00
Bowls, 11" & 12" Nappies	55.00
Bowls, Relish, Oval, 8" & 9"	30.00
Bowl, Relish, Oval, 12"	40.00
Candlesticks, 3½", Pr.	50.00
Candlesticks, 8½", Pr.	80.00
Candy Dish, ½ lb., Cone Shaped	55.00
Candy Dish & Cover, Three Feet	70.00
Celery Dish, 9"	35.00
Celery Dish, 12"	40.00
Cigarette Box	40.00
Cologne Bottle	40.00
Creamer, Footed or Flat	22.00
Cup	18.00
Decanter, 20 oz. w/Stopper	125.00
Demitasse Cup & Saucer	65.00
Egg Cup	36.00
Goblet, 2 oz. Wine	30.00
Goblet, 3 oz. Cocktail	20.00

	Pink or Green
Goblet, 6¼", 8 oz.	30.00
Grapefruit, 6½", Flange Rim	20.00
Lamp, 6¼", Electric	75.00
Lamp, 9¼"	125.00
Marmalade & Cover	40.00
Pitcher, 23 oz.	150.00
Pitcher, 39 oz.	210.00
Pitcher, 60 oz.	285.00
Pitcher, ½ Gal., Straight Sides	295.00
Plate, 5½" & 6½", Sherbet	8.00
Plate, 7¼", Pie	9.00
Plate, 8", Round or Square	12.00
Plate, 10", Dinner	32.50
Salt & Pepper, Pr., Round or Sq. Base	77.50
Salt Dip, 2" Footed & w/Place Card Holder	25.00
Saucer	4.00
Sherbet	14.00
Sugar, Footed or Flat	24.00
Tumbler, 3¾", 5 oz. or 8 oz.	20.00
Tumbler, 4", 10 oz. Iced Tea	25.00
Tumbler, 5", 12 oz. Iced Tea	30.00

FIRE-KING DINNERWARE "ALICE"
(Jade-ite, white/trim)
ANCHOR HOCKING COMPANY, 1940s

	Jade-ite	White/trim		Jade-ite	White/trim
Cup	7.00	12.00	Saucer	3.00	4.00
Plate	30.00	30.00			

FIRE-KING DINNERWARE "CHARM"

(Jade-ite, white/trim, Azur-ite, Forest Green, Royal Ruby)
ANCHOR HOCKING GLASS CORPORATION, 1940s – 1960s

	Azur-ite	Jade-ite		Azur-ite	Jade-ite
Bowl, 4¾", Dessert	6.00	14.00	Plate, 8⅜", Luncheon	8.50	15.00
Bowl, 6", Soup	15.00	35.00	Plate, 9¼", Dinner	22.00	45.00
Bowl, 7⅜", Salad	17.50	60.00	Platter	25.00	55.00
Creamer	12.00	20.00	Saucer	1.50	3.00
Cup	4.00	12.00	Sugar	12.00	20.00
Plate, 6⅝", Salad	9.00	25.00			

FIRE-KING DINNERWARE FLEURETTE

ANCHOR HOCKING GLASS CORPORATION, 1958 – 1960

	Fleurette		Fleurette
Bowl, 4⅝", Dessert	3.00	Plate, 7⅜", Salad	10.00
Bowl, 6⅝", Soup Plate	12.00	Plate, 9⅛", Dinner	5.00
Bowl, 8¼", Vegetable	11.00	Platter, 9" x 12"	14.00
Creamer	5.00	Saucer, 5¾"	1.00
Cup, 5 oz., Snack	3.00	Sugar	5.00
Cup, 8 oz	4.00	Sugar Cover	5.00
Plate, 6¼", Bread and Butter	14.00	Tray, 11"x 6", Snack	4.00

FIRE-KING DINNERWARE "GAME BIRDS" ⊂▭⊃
(white with decals)
ANCHOR HOCKING GLASS CORPORATION, 1959 – 1962

	White w/decals
Ashtray, 5¼"	18.00
Bowl, 4⅝", Dessert	5.00
Bowl, 5", Soup or Cereal	8.00
Bowl, 8¼", Vegetable	60.00
Creamer	20.00
Mug, 8 oz.	8.00
Plate, 6¼", Bread and Butter	10.00

	White w/decals
Plate, 9⅛", Dinner	6.50
Platter, 12" x 9"	50.00
Sugar	20.00
Sugar Cover	5.00
Tumbler, 5 oz., Juice	35.00
Tumbler, 11 oz., Iced Tea	12.00

FIRE-KING DINNERWARE GRAY LAUREL
ANCHOR HOCKING GLASS CORPORATION, 1952 – 1963

	Gray Laurel		Gray Laurel
Bowl, 4⅞", Dessert	7.00	Plate, 7⅜", Salad	8.00
Bowl, 7⅝", Soup Plate	16.00	Plate, 9⅛", Dinner	10.00
Bowl, 8¼", Vegetable	30.00	Plate, 11", Serving	20.00
Creamer, Ftd.	5.00	Saucer, 5¾"	3.00
Cup, 8 oz.	4.00	Sugar, Ftd.	5.00

FIRE-KING DINNERWARE HONEYSUCKLE
(white with decals)
ANCHOR HOCKING GLASS CORPORATION, 1958 – 1960

	White w/decals		White w/decals
Bowl, 4⅝", Dessert	4.00	Platter, 9" x 12"	16.00
Bowl, 6⅝", Soup Plate	9.00	Saucer, 5¾"	1.50
Bowl, 8¼", Vegetable	15.00	Sugar	5.00
Creamer	5.00	Sugar Cover	5.00
Cup, 8 oz.	4.00	Tumbler, 5 oz., Juice	18.00
Plate 6¼", Bread & Butter	15.00	Tumbler, 9 oz., Water	15.00
Plate, 7⅜", Salad	5.00	Tumbler, 12 oz., Iced Tea	15.00
Plate, 9⅛", Dinner	6.00		

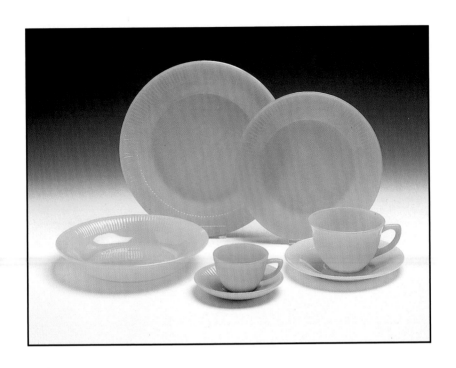

FIRE-KING DINNERWARE "JANE RAY"
(Jade-ite, Vitrock, white)
ANCHOR HOCKING COMPANY, 1945 – 1960s

	Jade-ite		Jade-ite
Bowl, 4⅞", Dessert	10.00	Plate, 7¾", Salad	12.00
Bowl, 5⅞", Oatmeal	20.00	Plate, 9⅛", Dinner	13.00
Bowl, 7⅝", Soup	24.00	Platter, 12"	25.00
Bowl, 8¼", Vegetable	25.00	Saucer	2.00
Cup	6.00	Saucer, Demitasse	45.00
Cup, Demitasse	40.00	Sugar	10.00
Creamer	9.00	Sugar Cover	22.50

FIRE-KING DINNERWARE PEACH LUSTRE ⊂⊃
ANCHOR HOCKING GLASS CORPORATION, 1952 – 1963

	Peach Lustre
Bowl, 4⅞", Dessert	4.00
Bowl, 7⅝", Soup Plate	10.00
Bowl, 8¼", Vegetable	10.00
Creamer, Ftd.	4.00
Cup, 8 oz.	3.50

	Peach Lustre
Plate, 7⅜", Salad	9.00
Plate, 9⅛", Dinner	5.00
Plate, 11", Serving	14.00
Saucer, 5¾"	1.00
Sugar, Ftd.	4.00

FIRE-KING DINNERWARE "PHILBE"
(blue, pink, green, and crystal)
ANCHOR HOCKING GLASS COMPANY, 1937 – 1938

	Pink or Green		Pink or Green
Bowl, 5½", Cereal	45.00	Plate, 10½", Salver	75.00
Bowl, 7¼", Salad	80.00	Plate, 10½", Grill	75.00
Bowl, 10", Oval Vegetable	90.00	Plate, 11⅝", Salver	62.50
Candy Jar, 4", Low w/Cover	725.00	Platter, 12", Closed Handles	125.00
Cookie Jar w/Cover	950.00	Saucer, 6" (same as sherbet	
Creamer, 3¼", Footed	135.00	plate)	65.00
Cup	110.00	Sugar, 3¼", Footed	135.00
Goblet, 7¼", Thin, 9 oz.	185.00	Tumbler, 4", 9 oz., Flat Water	105.00
Pitcher, 6", Juice, 36 oz.	625.00	Tumbler, 3½", Footed Juice	150.00
Pitcher, 8½", 54 oz.	925.00	Tumbler, 5¼", Footed, 10 oz.	80.00
Plate, 6", Sherbet	65.00	Tumbler, 6½", Footed, 15 oz.	
Plate, 8", Luncheon	37.50	Iced Tea	85.00
Plate, 10", Heavy Sandwich	75.00		

FIRE-KING DINNERWARE & OVENWARE PRIMROSE
(white with decal)
ANCHOR HOCKING GLASS CORPORATION, 1960 – 1962

White w/decal

Bowl, 4⅝", Dessert	3.50
Bowl, 6⅝", Soup Plate	9.00
Bowl, 8¼", Vegetable	14.00
Cake pan, 8", Round	12.00
Cake pan, 8", Square	12.00
Casserole, pt., Knob Cover	9.00
Casserole, ½ qt., Oval, Au Gratin cover	15.00
Casserole, 1 qt., Knob Cover	12.00
Casserole, 1½ qt., Knob Cover	12.00
Casserole, 2 qt., Knob Cover	16.00
Creamer	5.00
Cup, 5 oz., Snack	3.00
Cup, 8 oz.	3.00
Custard, 6 oz., Low or Dessert	3.50

White w/decal

Pan, 5" x 9", Baking, w/Cover	18.00
Pan, 5" x 9", Deep Loaf	14.00
Pan, 6½" x 10½", Utility Baking	12.00
Pan, 8" x 12½", Utility Baking	25.00
Plate, 7⅜", Salad	5.00
Plate, 9⅛", Dinner	7.00
Platter, 9" x 12"	15.00
Saucer, 5¾"	1.00
Sugar	5.00
Sugar Cover	5.00
Tray, 11" x 6", Rectangular, Snack	5.00
Tumbler, 5 oz., Juice (White)	30.00
Tumbler, 10 oz., Iced Tea (Crystal)	50.00
Tumbler, 11 oz., Water (White)	25.00

FIRE-KING OVEN GLASS
(blue, 1940s; crystal, 1950s)
ANCHOR HOCKING GLASS COMPANY

	Blue		**Blue**
Baker, 1 pt., Round or Square......	7.00	Loaf Pan, 9⅛" Deep	22.00
Baker, 1 qt.	11.00	Nurser, 4 oz.	20.00
Baker, 1½ qt.	15.00	Nurser, 8 oz.	35.00
Baker, 2 qt.	15.00	Pie Plate, 4⅜", Individual..............	21.00
Cake Pan (no tabs), 8¾"..............	40.00	Pie Plate, 5⅜", Deep Dish	22.00
Casserole, 1 pt., Knob Handle		Pie Plate, 8⅜"	9.00
Cover	13.00	Pie Plate, 9"	10.00
Casserole, 1 qt., Knob Handle		Pie Plate, 9⅝"	10.00
Cover	17.00	Pie Plate, 10⅜", Juice Saver	150.00
Casserole, 1½ qt., Knob Handle		Percolator Top, 2⅛"......................	5.00
Cover	21.00	Refrigerator Jar & Cover, 4½" x 5".	15.00
Casserole, 2 qt., Knob Handle		Refrigerator Jar & Cover,	
Cover	21.00	5⅛" x 9⅛".................................	32.50
Casserole, 1 qt., Pie Plate Cover..	18.00	Roaster, 8¾"	55.00
Casserole, 1½ qt., Pie Plate		Roaster, 10⅜"	80.00
Cover	20.00	Table Server, Tab Handles	
Casserole, 2 qt., Pie Plate Cover..	25.00	(Hot Plate).................................	22.00
Casserole, 10 oz., Tab Handle		Utility Bowl, 6⅞"	17.00
Cover	13.00	Utility Bowl, 8⅜"	19.00
Coffee Mug, 7 oz.	26.00	Utility Bowl, 10⅛"	21.00
Cup, 8 oz., Measuring	20.00	Utility Pan, 10½" x 2" deep	25.00
Custard Cup, 5 oz.........................	4.00	Utility Pan, 8⅛" x 12½".................	100.00
Custard Cup, 6 oz., Two Styles....	5.00		

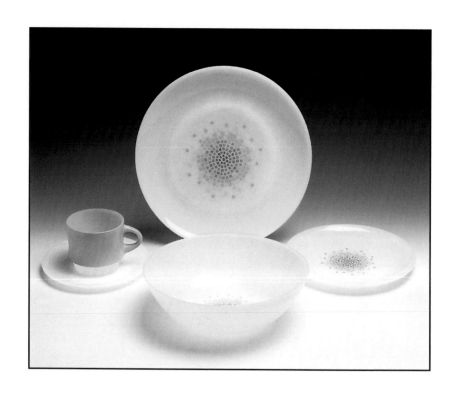

FIRE-KING OVEN WARE BLUE MOSAIC ⊂⎯⎯⎯⎯⊃
ANCHOR HOCKING GLASS CORPORATION, 1962 – Late 1960s

	Blue Mosaic
Bowl, 4⅝", Dessert	8.00
Bowl, 6⅝", Soup Plate	14.00
Bowl, 8¼", Vegetable	18.00
Creamer	8.00
Cup, 7½ oz.	4.00
Plate, 7⅜", Salad	8.00

	Blue Mosaic
Plate, 10", Dinner	10.00
Platter, 9" x 12"	17.50
Saucer, 5¾"	2.00
Sugar	8.00
Sugar Cover	5.00
Tray, 10" x 7½", Oval, Snack	6.00

FIRE-KING OVEN WARE
TURQUOISE BLUE
(turquoise blue)
ANCHOR HOCKING GLASS CORPORATION, 1950s

	Blue		Blue
Ashtray, 3½"	9.00	Bowl, Round, Mixing, 2 qt.	22.00
Ashtray, 4⅝"	11.00	Bowl, Round, Mixing, 3 qt.	24.00
Ashtray, 5¾"	15.00	Creamer	8.00
Batter Bowl, w/Spout	300.00	Cup	5.00
Bowl, 4½", Berry	10.00	Mug, 8 oz.	10.00
Bowl, 5", Cereal	15.00	Plate, 6⅛"	18.00
Bowl, 6⅝", Soup/Salad	25.00	Plate, 7¼"	12.00
Bowl, 8", Vegetable	22.00	Plate, 9"	12.00
Bowl, Tear, Mixing, 1 pt.	30.00	Plate, 9" w/Cup Indent	6.00
Bowl, Tear, Mixing, 1 qt.	35.00	Plate, 10"	30.00
Bowl, Tear, Mixing, 2 qt.	35.00	Relish, 3-Part	12.00
Bowl, Tear, Mixing, 3 qt.	60.00	Saucer	1.50
Bowl, Round, Mixing, 1 qt.	20.00	Sugar	8.00

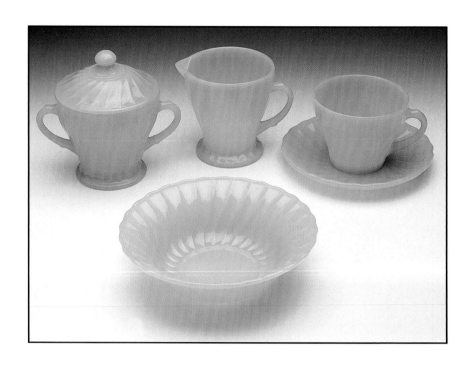

FIRE-KING OVEN WARE "SHELL," 1960s ⊂══════⊃
(Jade-ite, lustre, white)
ANCHOR HOCKING GLASS CORPORATION, 1960s – 1975

	Jade-ite "Shell"	Lustre "Shell"		Jade-ite "Shell"	Lustre "Shell"
Bowl, 4¾", Dessert	12.00	4.00	Saucer, 4¾", Demitasse	----	10.00
Bowl, 6⅜", Cereal	25.00	10.00	Plate, 7¼", Salad	18.00	5.00
Bowl, 7⅝", Soup Plate	30.00	15.00	Plate, 10", Dinner	25.00	7.00
Bowl, 8½", Vegetable	28.00	18.00	Platter, 9½" x 13"	85.00	----
Creamer, Ftd.	25.00	10.00	Saucer, 5¾"	4.00	2.00
Cup, 8 oz.	10.00	5.00	Sugar, Ftd.	25.00	10.00
Cup, 3¼ oz., Demitasse	----	10.00	Sugar Cover	75.00	8.00

FIRE-KING OVEN WARE SUNRISE

ANCHOR HOCKING GLASS CORPORATION

	Sunrise			Sunrise
Bowl, 4⅞", Fruit or Dessert	5.00	Plate, 9⅛", Dinner		10.00
Bowl, 7⅝", Soup Plate	20.00	Platter, 12" x 9"		18.00
Bowl, 8¼", Vegetable	25.00	Saucer, 5¾"		2.00
Creamer, Flat	10.00	Sugar Lid, for Flat Sugar		12.00
Cup, 8 oz.	6.50	Sugar, Flat, Tab Handles		12.00
Plate, 7⅜", Salad	8.00			

FIRE-KING OVEN WARE WHEAT
ANCHOR HOCKING GLASS CORPORATION, 1962 – Late 1960s

	Wheat
Bowl, 4⅝", Dessert	3.50
Bowl, 6⅝", Soup plate	8.00
Bowl, 8¼", Vegetable	12.00
Cake pan, 8", Round	11.00
Cake pan, 8", Square	10.00
Casserole, 1 pt., Knob Cover	8.00
Casserole, 1 qt., Knob Cover	10.00
Casserole, 1½ qt., Knob Cover	11.00
Casserole, 1½ qt., Oval, Au Gratin Cover	14.00
Casserole, 2 qt., Knob Cover	15.00
Creamer	5.00
Cup, 5 oz., Snack	3.00
Cup, 8 oz.	4.00

	Wheat
Custard, 6 oz., Low or Dessert	3.00
Pan, 5" x 9", Baking, w/Cover	16.00
Pan, 5" x 9", Deep Loaf	12.00
Pan, 6½" x 10½" x 1½", Utility Baking	12.00
Pan, 8" x 12½" x 2", Utility Baking	18.00
Plate, 7⅜", Salad	6.00
Plate, 10", Dinner	6.00
Platter, 9" x 12"	14.00
Saucer, 5¾"	1.00
Sugar	4.50
Sugar Cover	4.00
Tray, 11" x 6", Rectangular, Snack.	4.00

FLORAGOLD "LOUISA"
(iridescent, Shell Pink, crystal)
JEANNETTE GLASS COMPANY, 1950s

	Iridescent		Iridescent
Bowl, 4½", Square	5.50	Cup	6.00
Bowl, 5½", Cereal, Round	40.00	Pitcher, 64 oz.	38.00
Bowl, 5½", Ruffled Fruit	8.00	Plate, 5¾", Sherbet	12.00
Bowl, 8½", Square	14.00	Plate, 8½", Dinner	40.00
Bowl, 9½", Salad, Deep	45.00	Plate or Tray, 13½"	22.00
Bowl, 9½", Ruffled	9.00	Indent on 13½" Plate	65.00
Bowl, 12", Ruffled, Large Fruit	8.00	Platter, 11¼"	25.00
Butter Dish & Cover, ¼ lb.,		Salt & Pepper, Plastic Tops	55.00
Oblong	25.00	Saucer (same as Sherbet Plate)	12.00
Butter Dish & Cover, Round	45.00	Sherbet, Low Footed	16.00
Candlesticks, Double Branch, Pr.	55.00	Sugar	6.50
Candy or Cheese Dish & Cover,		Sugar Lid	12.00
6¾"	55.00	Tumbler, 10 oz., Footed	20.00
Candy, 5¼" Long, 4 Feet	7.50	Tumbler, 11 oz., Footed	20.00
Coaster/Ashtray, 4"	5.50	Tumbler, 15 oz., Footed	115.00
Creamer	9.00	Vase or Celery	435.00

FLORAL, "POINSETTIA"
(See Reproduction Section, Page 174)
(pink, green, delphite)
JEANNETTE GLASS COMPANY, 1931 – 1935

	Pink	Green
Bowl, 4", Berry	20.00	22.00
Bowl, 5½", Cream Soup	750.00	750.00
Bowl, 7½", Salad	30.00	30.00
Bowl, 8", Covered Vegetable	55.00	65.00
Bowl, 9", Oval Vegetable	24.00	26.00
Butter Dish & Cover	100.00	90.00
Candlesticks, 4", Pr.	90.00	95.00
Candy Jar & Cover	45.00	43.00
Coaster, 3¼"	15.00	14.00
Compote, 9"	900.00	995.00
Creamer, Flat	18.00	20.00
Cup	14.00	14.00
Ice Tub, 3½" High, Oval	900.00	950.00
Lamp	250.00	275.00
Pitcher, 5½", 23 or 24 oz., Flat	----	550.00
Pitcher, 8", 32 oz., Footed Cone	35.00	45.00
Pitcher, 10¼", 48 oz., Lemonade	250.00	275.00
Plate, 6", Sherbet	8.00	9.00
Plate, 8", Salad	14.00	16.00
Plate, 9", Dinner	20.00	22.00

	Pink	Green
Plate, 9", Grill	----	295.00
Platter, 10¾", Oval	22.00	24.00
Refrigerator Dish & Cover, 5" Square	----	75.00
Relish Dish, Oval, Two-Part	22.00	24.00
Salt & Pepper, 4", Footed, Pr. (Beware reproductions)	50.00	55.00
Salt & Pepper, 6" Flat	55.00	----
Saucer	12.00	12.00
Sherbet	20.00	20.00
Sugar	10.00	12.00
Sugar/Candy Cover	15.00	20.00
Tray, 6" Square, Closed Handles	18.00	20.00
Tumbler, 4", 5 oz., Footed Juice	18.00	25.00
Tumbler, 4¾", 7 oz., Footed Water	22.00	24.00
Tumbler, 5¼", 9 oz., Footed Lemonade	55.00	60.00
Vase, 3-Legged Rose Bowl	----	525.00
Vase, 3-Legged Flared (Also in Crystal)	----	495.00
Vase, 6⅞" Tall (8-sided)	----	450.00

FLORAL AND DIAMOND BAND

(crystal, pink, green)
U.S. GLASS COMPANY, 1927 – 1931

	Pink	Green
Bowl, 4½", Berry	10.00	12.00
Bowl, 5¾", Nappy, Handled	15.00	15.00
Bowl, 8", Large Berry	20.00	20.00
Butter Dish & Cover	140.00	130.00
Compote, 5½" Tall	17.00	20.00
Creamer, Small	10.00	12.00
Creamer, 4¾"	18.00	20.00

	Pink	Green
Pitcher, 8", 42 oz.	115.00	125.00
Plate, 8", Luncheon	45.00	45.00
Sherbet	7.00	8.00
Sugar, Small	10.00	12.00
Sugar, 5¼"	18.00	18.00
Sugar Lid	55.00	65.00
Tumbler, 4", Water	25.00	25.00
Tumbler, 5", Iced Tea	40.00	50.00

FLORENTINE NO. 1, "POPPY NO. 1"
(See Reproduction Section, Page 173)
(pink, green, crystal, yellow, cobalt)
HAZEL ATLAS GLASS COMPANY, 1934 – 1936

	Green	Yellow
Ashtray, 5½"	22.00	30.00
Bowl, 5", Berry	12.00	15.00
Bowl, 6", Cereal	25.00	30.00
Bowl, 8½", Large Berry	25.00	35.00
Bowl, 9½", Oval Vegetable & Cover	55.00	75.00
Butter Dish & Cover	125.00	160.00
Coaster/Ashtray, 3¾"	18.00	20.00
Creamer	10.00	18.00
Creamer, Ruffled	45.00	----
Cup	9.00	10.00
Pitcher, 6½", 36 oz., Footed	40.00	45.00
Pitcher, 7½", 54 oz., Flat Ice Lip or None	75.00	195.00
Plate, 6", Sherbet	6.00	7.00

	Green	Yellow
Plate, 8½", Salad	8.00	12.00
Plate, 10", Dinner	18.00	25.00
Plate, 10", Grill	12.00	15.00
Platter, 11½", Oval	20.00	25.00
* Salt & Pepper, Footed	37.50	55.00
Saucer	3.00	4.00
Sherbet, 3 oz., Footed	11.00	14.00
Sugar	10.00	13.00
Sugar Cover	18.00	30.00
Sugar, Ruffled	40.00	----
Tumbler, 3¾", 5 oz., Footed Juice	16.00	25.00
Tumbler, 4¾", 10 oz., Footed Water	22.00	24.00
Tumbler, 5¼", 12 oz., Footed Iced Tea	28.00	30.00

* Beware reproductions

FLORENTINE NO. 2, "POPPY NO. 2"
(See Reproduction section page 174)
(pink, green, yellow, crystal, cobalt blue)
HAZEL ATLAS GLASS COMPANY, 1932 – 1935

	Green	Yellow
Bowl, 4½", Berry	14.00	22.00
Bowl, 4¾", Cream Soup	16.00	22.00
Bowl, 5½"	35.00	45.00
Bowl, 6", Cereal	33.00	42.00
Bowl, 8", Large Berry	25.00	35.00
Bowl, 9", Oval Vegetable & Cover	65.00	85.00
Butter Dish & Cover	110.00	160.00
Candlesticks, 2¾", Pr.	50.00	70.00
Candy Dish & Cover	110.00	165.00
Coaster, 3¼"	14.00	22.00
Coaster/Ashtray, 3¾"	18.00	30.00
Coaster/Ashtray, 5½"	17.50	40.00
Compote, 3½", Ruffled	40.00	----
Creamer	8.00	10.00
Cup	8.00	10.00
Custard Cup or Jello	60.00	85.00
Gravy Boat	----	65.00
Pitcher, 7½", 28 oz., Cone Footed	35.00	35.00
Pitcher, 7½", 48 oz.	75.00	250.00
Pitcher, 8", 76 oz.	110.00	450.00
Plate, 6", Sherbet	4.00	6.00

	Green	Yellow
Plate, 6¼", w/Indent for Custard	20.00	30.00
Plate, 8½", Salad	9.00	10.00
Plate, 10", Dinner	16.00	16.00
Plate, 10¼", Grill	14.00	18.00
Platter, 11", Oval	16.00	22.50
Platter, 11½" for Gravy Boat	----	45.00
Relish Dish, 10", 3 Part or Plain	22.00	32.00
Salt & Pepper, Pr.	42.50	50.00
Saucer	4.00	5.00
Sherbet, Footed	12.00	13.00
Sugar	10.00	12.00
Sugar Cover	15.00	28.00
Tumbler, 3½", 5 oz., Juice	14.00	22.00
Tumbler, 4", 9 oz. Water	13.00	22.00
Tumbler, 5", 12 oz., Iced Tea	38.00	55.00
Tumbler, 3¼", 5 oz., Footed	15.00	18.00
Tumbler, 4", 5 oz., Footed	15.00	17.00
Tumbler, 4½", 9 oz., Footed	30.00	35.00
Vase or Parfait, 6"	35.00	65.00

FLOWER GARDEN WITH BUTTERFLIES, "BUTTERFLIES AND ROSES"

(pink, green, blue-green, canary yellow, amber, black)
U.S. GLASS COMPANY, Late 1920s

	Pink or Green		Pink or Green
Ashtray, Match-Pack Holders	190.00	Plate, 8", Two Styles	18.00
Candlesticks, 4", Pr.	55.00	Plate, 10"	45.00
Candlesticks, 8", Pr.	145.00	Powder Jar, Footed	145.00
Candy Dish & Cover, 7½"	135.00	Powder Jar, Flat	80.00
Candy Dish, Open, 6"	30.00	Sandwich Server, Center Handle	75.00
Cheese & Cracker Set (4" Compote, 10" Plate)	75.00	Saucer	25.00
Cologne Bottle, 7½", Tall Footed	200.00	Sugar, Open	75.00
Console Bowl, 10" Footed	85.00	Tray, 5½" x 10", Oval	60.00
Creamer	75.00	Tray, Rectangular, 11¾" x 7¾"	65.00
Cup	70.00	Vase, 7", (black)	165.00
		Vase, 10½"	135.00

FOREST GREEN

(dark green glass)
ANCHOR HOCKING, 1950s – 1967

	Green		Green
Ashtray	5.00	Pitcher, 3 Qt., Round	40.00
Bowl, 4¾", Dessert	6.00	Platter, Rectangular	24.00
Bowl, 6", Soup	20.00	Saucer	1.50
Bowl, 7⅜", Salad	15.00	Sugar, Flat	6.50
Creamer, Flat	6.50	Tumbler, 5 oz	4.00
Cup	5.00	Tumbler, 10 oz	7.00
Plate, 6⅝", Salad	5.00	Vase, 4", Ivy	5.00
Plate, 8⅜", Luncheon	7.00	Vase, 6⅜"	6.00
Plate, 9¼", Dinner	30.00	Vase, 9"	12.00

"FORTUNE"
(pink, crystal)
HOCKING GLASS COMPANY, 1937 – 1938

	Pink		Pink
Bowl, 4", Berry	8.00	Cup	10.00
Bowl, 4½", Dessert	10.00	Plate, 6", Sherbet	5.00
Bowl, 4½", Handled	10.00	Plate, 8", Luncheon	25.00
Bowl, 5¼", Rolled Edge	18.00	Saucer	4.00
Bowl, 7¾", Salad or Large Berry	22.00	Tumbler, 3½", Juice, 5 oz.	10.00
Candy Dish & Cover, Flat	25.00	Tumbler, 4", Water, 9 oz.	12.00

"FRUITS"

(pink, green, crystal)

HAZEL ATLAS AND OTHER GLASS COMPANIES, 1931 – 1953

	Pink	Green
Bowl, 5", Cereal	25.00	32.00
Bowl, 8", Berry	45.00	85.00
Cup	7.00	8.00
Pitcher, 7", Flat Bottom	----	90.00
Plate, 8", Luncheon	10.00	10.00
Saucer	4.00	6.00

	Pink	Green
Sherbet	10.00	12.00
Tumbler, 3½", Juice	----	60.00
Tumbler, 4" (One Fruit)	18.00	20.00
Tumbler, 4" (Combination of Fruits)	22.00	28.00
Tumbler, 5", 12 oz.	----	165.00

GEORGIAN, "LOVEBIRDS"
(green, crystal)
FEDERAL GLASS COMPANY, 1931 – 1936

	Green
Bowl, 4½", Berry	10.00
Bowl, 5¾", Cereal	25.00
Bowl, 6½", Deep	70.00
Bowl, 7½", Large Berry	63.00
Bowl, 9", Oval Vegetable	63.00
Butter Dish & Cover	85.00
Cold Cuts Server, 18½", Wood w/Seven 5" Openings for 5" Coasters	900.00
Creamer, 3", Footed	12.00
Creamer, 4", Footed	17.00
Cup	10.00
Hot Plate, 5" Center Design	50.00

	Green
Plate, 6", Sherbet	7.00
Plate, 8", Luncheon	12.00
Plate, 9¼", Dinner	25.00
Plate, 9¼", Center Design Only	22.00
Platter, 11½", Closed Handled	68.00
Saucer	3.00
Sherbet	12.00
Sugar, 3", Footed	10.00
Sugar, 4", Footed	12.00
Sugar Cover, 3"	45.00
Tumbler, 4", Flat, 9 oz.	65.00
Tumbler, 5¼", Flat, 12 oz.	135.00

GOLDEN GLORY
FEDERAL GLASS COMPANY, 1959 – 1966; 1978 – 1979

Bowl, 4⅞", Dessert	4.50	Plate, 10", Dinner	6.50
Bowl, 6⅜", Soup	8.00	Platter, 11¼", Round	15.00
Bowl, 8½", Vegetable	12.00	Platter, 12", Oval	11.00
Bowl, 8", Rimmed Soup	10.00	Saucer	.50
Creamer	4.00	Sugar	3.00
Cup	3.00	Sugar Lid	4.00
Plate, 7⅜", Salad	3.00	Tumbler, 9 oz., Ftd.	10.00
Plate, 9⅛", Dinner	5.00	Tumbler, 10 oz., 5"	10.00

HARP

(crystal and crystal with gold rims)
JEANNETTE GLASS COMPANY, 1954 – 1957

	Crystal		Crystal
Ashtray/Coaster	5.00	Plate, 7"	15.00
Coaster	4.50	Saucer	12.50
Cup	32.50	Tray, Rectangular	35.00
Cake Stand, 9"	25.00	Vase, 6"	25.00

HERITAGE
(crystal, pink, blue, green)
FEDERAL GLASS COMPANY, Late 1930s – 1960s

	Crystal		Crystal
Bowl, 5", Berry	8.00	Plate, 8", Luncheon	9.00
Bowl, 8½", Large Berry	40.00	Plate, 9¼", Dinner	12.00
Bowl, 10½", Fruit	15.00	Plate, 12", Sandwich	15.00
Cup	7.00	Saucer	4.00
Creamer, Footed	30.00	Sugar, Open, Footed	25.00

HEX OPTIC, "HONEYCOMB"
(pink, green)
JEANNETTE GLASS COMPANY, 1928 – 1932

	Pink or Green		Pink or Green
Bowl, 4¼", Berry, Ruffled	7.00	Plate, 8", Luncheon	6.00
Bowl, 7½", Large Berry	10.00	Platter, 11", Round	15.00
Butter Dish & Cover, Rectangular,		Refrigerator Dish, 4" x 4"	12.00
1 lb. size	90.00	Salt & Pepper, Pr.	27.50
Bucket Reamer	55.00	Saucer	2.50
Creamer, Two Style Handles	6.00	Sugar, Two Styles of Handles	6.00
Cup, Two Style Handles	4.50	Sugar Shaker	225.00
Ice Bucket, Metal Handle	20.00	Sherbet, 5 oz., Footed	4.50
Pitcher, 5", 32 oz., Sunflower		Tumbler, 3¾", 9 oz.	4.50
Motif in Bottom	22.00	Tumbler, 5¾", Footed	10.00
Pitcher, 9", 48 oz., Footed	50.00	Tumbler, 7", Footed	12.00
Plate, 6", Sherbet	2.50	Whiskey, 2", 1 oz.	8.00

HOBNAIL
(crystal, pink)
HOCKING GLASS COMPANY, 1934 – 1936

	Crystal		Crystal
Bowl, 5½", Cereal	4.00	Plate, 8½", Luncheon	3.50
Bowl, 7", Salad	5.00	Saucer	2.00
Cup	4.50	Sherbet	3.00
Creamer, Footed	4.00	Sugar, Footed	4.00
Decanter & Stopper, 32 oz.	32.00	Tumbler, Juice, 5 oz.	4.00
Goblet, Water, 10 oz.	8.00	Tumbler, Water, 9 oz., 10 oz.	5.50
Goblet, Iced Tea, 13 oz.	10.00	Tumbler, Iced Tea, 15 oz.	15.00
Pitcher, Milk, 18 oz.	20.00	Tumbler, Footed Wine, 3 oz.	7.00
Pitcher, 67 oz.	25.00	Tumbler, Footed Cordial, 5 oz.	6.00
Plate, 6", Sherbet	2.00	Whiskey, 1½ oz.	7.00

HOLIDAY, "BUTTON AND BOWS"
(pink, iridescent)
JEANNETTE GLASS COMPANY, 1947 – 1949

	Pink		Pink
Bowl, 5⅛", Berry	13.00	Plate, 6", Sherbet	6.00
Bowl, 7¾", Soup	55.00	Plate, 9", Dinner	17.00
Bowl, 8½", Large Berry	30.00	Plate, 13¾", Chop	110.00
Bowl, 9½", Oval Vegetable	28.00	Platter, 11⅜", Oval	20.00
Bowl, 10¾", Console	135.00	Sandwich Tray, 10½"	17.50
Butter Dish & Cover	40.00	Saucer, Two Style	4.00
Cake Plate, 10½", Three-Legged	110.00	Sherbet	6.00
Candlesticks, 3", Pr.	110.00	Sugar	10.00
Creamer, Footed	8.00	Sugar Cover	15.00
Cup, Two Sizes	8.00	Tumbler, 4", 10 oz., Flat	23.00
Pitcher, 4¾", Milk, 16 oz.	65.00	Tumbler, 4", Footed	45.00
Pitcher, 6¾", 52 oz.	38.00	Tumbler, 6", Footed	160.00

HOMESPUN, "FINE RIB"
(pink, crystal)
JEANNETTE GLASS COMPANY, 1939 – 1940

	Pink		Pink
Bowl, 4½", Closed Handles	15.00	Tumbler, 4", Water, 9 oz.	20.00
Bowl, 5", Cereal	28.00	Tumbler, 5¼", Iced Tea, 13 oz.	33.00
Bowl, 8¼", Large Berry	24.00	Tumbler, 4", 5 oz., Footed	7.00
Butter Dish & Cover	60.00	Tumbler, 6¼", 15 oz., Footed	33.00
Coaster/Ashtray	6.50	Tumbler, 6⅜", 15 oz., Footed	33.00
Creamer, Footed	12.50		
Cup	11.00		
Plate, 6", Sherbet	6.00	**CHILD'S TEA SET**	
Plate, 9¼", Dinner	22.00	Cup	35.00
Platter, 13", Closed Handles	20.00	Saucer	11.00
Saucer	4.00	Plate	14.00
Sherbet, Low Flat	18.00	Teapot	55.00
Sugar, Footed	12.50	Teapot Cover	80.00
Tumbler, 3⅞", 6 oz.	22.00	Set of 14 Pieces	375.00

INDIANA CUSTARD, "FLOWER AND LEAF BAND"

(ivory or custard, early 1930s; white, 1950s)
INDIANA GLASS COMPANY

	Ivory
Bowl, 5½", Berry	12.00
Bowl, 6½", Cereal	28.00
Bowl, 7½", Flat Soup	35.00
Bowl, 9", Large Berry	35.00
Bowl, 9½", Oval Vegetable	33.00
Butter Dish & Cover	65.00
Cup	37.50
Creamer	17.50
Plate, 5¾", Bread & Butter	6.50

	Ivory
Plate, 7½", Salad	18.00
Plate, 8⅞", Luncheon	18.00
Plate, 9¾", Dinner	30.00
Platter, 11½", Oval	40.00
Saucer	8.00
Sherbet	100.00
Sugar	12.00
Sugar Cover	25.00

IRIS, "IRIS AND HERRINGBONE"

(See Reproduction Section, Page 175)
(crystal, iridescent)
JEANNETTE GLASS COMPANY, 1928 – 1932; 1950; 1970

	Crystal	Iridescent		Crystal	Iridescent
Bowl, 4½", Berry,			Demitasse Saucer	145.00	250.00
Beaded	45.00	10.00	Goblet, 4", Wine	----	30.00
Bowl, 5", Sauce	9.00	28.00	Goblet, 4½", Wine	17.00	----
Bowl, 5", Cereal	125.00	----	Goblet, 5½", 4 oz.	28.00	250.00
Bowl, 7½", Soup	165.00	60.00	Goblet, 5½", 8 oz.	26.00	250.00
Bowl, 8", Large Berry,			Pitcher, 9½", Footed	40.00	42.50
Beaded	85.00	25.00	Plate, 5½", Sherbet	15.00	14.00
Bowl, 9½", Salad	12.50	13.00	Plate, 8", Luncheon	110.00	----
Bowl, 11", Fruit,			Plate, 9", Dinner	55.00	48.00
Ruffled	15.00	14.00	Plate, 11¾", Sandwich.	33.00	33.00
Bowl, 11", Fruit,			Saucer	12.00	11.00
Straight	65.00	----	Sherbet, 2½", Footed.	28.00	15.00
Butter Dish & Cover	47.50	45.00	Sherbet, 4", Footed	28.00	225.00
Candlesticks, Pr.	45.00	48.00	Sugar	11.00	11.00
Candy Jar & Cover	175.00	----	Sugar Cover	12.00	12.00
Coaster	110.00	----	Tumbler, 4", Flat	150.00	----
Creamer, Footed	12.00	12.00	Tumbler, 6", Footed	18.00	18.00
Cup	15.00	14.00	Tumbler, 6½", Footed	25.00	----
Demitasse Cup	35.00	150.00	Vase, 9"	27.50	25.00

JAMESTOWN

(amber, amethyst, blue, brown, crystal, green, pink, red)
FOSTORIA GLASS COMPANY, 1958 – 1982

	Amber	Ruby
Bowl, 4½", Dessert #2719/421	8.50	16.00
Bowl, 10", Salad #2719//211	21.00	50.00
Bowl, 10", Two Hndl. Serving #2719/648	21.00	60.00
Butter w/Cover, ¼ pound #2719/300	24.00	60.00
Cake Plate, 9½", Hndl. #2719/306	16.00	40.00
Celery, 9¼" #2719/360	18.00	37.50
Cream, 3½", Ftd. #2719/681	11.00	25.00
Jelly w/Cover, 6⅛" #2719/447	32.50	80.00
Pickle, 8⅜" #2719/540	21.00	45.00
Pitcher, 7⁵⁄₁₆", 48 oz., Ice Jug #2719/456	45.00	135.00
Plate, 8" #2719/550	8.50	23.00
Plate, 14", Torte #2719/567	26.00	60.00
Relish, 9⅛", 2 Part #2719/620	16.00	37.50
Salad Set, 4 Pc. (10" Bowl, 14" Plate w/Wood Fork & Spoon) #2719/286	55.00	100.00
Salver, 7" High, 10" Diameter #2719/630	60.00	120.00
Sauce Dish w/Cover, 4½" #2719/635	18.00	40.00
Shaker, 3½", w/Chrome Top. Pr. #2719/653	26.00	50.00
Stem, 4⁵⁄₁₆", 4 oz., Wine #2719/26	10.00	25.00
*Stem, 4¼", 6½ oz., Sherbet #2719/7	6.50	16.00
*Stem, 4⅛", 7 oz., Sherbet #2719/7	6.50	16.00
*Stem, 5¾", 9½ oz., Goblet #2719/2	10.00	16.00
*Stem, 5⅞", 10 oz., Goblet #2719/2	10.00	16.00
Sugar, 3½", Ftd. #2719/679	11.00	25.00
Tray, 9⅜", Hndl. Muffin #2719/726	26.00	55.00
Tumbler, 4¼", 9 oz. #2719/73	9.00	25.00
Tumbler, 4¾", 5 oz., Juice #2719/88	9.50	26.00
Tumbler, 5⅛", 12 oz. #2719/64	9.00	26.00
Tumbler, 6", 11 oz., Ftd. Tea #2719/63	10.00	24.00
Tumbler, 6", 12 oz., Ftd. Tea #2719/63	10.00	24.00

*being remade at present

JUBILEE

(yellow, pink, crystal)
LANCASTER GLASS COMPANY, Early 1930s

	Pink	Yellow
Bowl, 8", 3-Ftd., 5⅛" High	250.00	200.00
Bowl, 9" Handled Fruit	----	125.00
Bowl, 11½", Flat Fruit	195.00	160.00
Bowl, 11½", 3-Ftd.	250.00	250.00
Bowl, 11½", 3-Ftd., Curved In	----	225.00
Bowl, 13", 3-Ftd.	250.00	225.00
Candlestick, Pr.	185.00	185.00
Candy Jar, w/Lid, 3-Ftd.	325.00	325.00
Cheese & Cracker Set	255.00	265.00
Creamer	35.00	18.00
Cup	40.00	13.00
Mayonnaise & Plate	295.00	250.00
w/Original Ladle	310.00	265.00
Plate, 7" Salad	22.50	14.00
Plate, 8¾" Luncheon	25.00	12.00
Plate, 13½" Sandwich	85.00	50.00
Plate, 14", 3-Ftd.	----	200.00

	Pink	Yellow
Saucer, Two Styles	12.00	4.00
Sherbet, 3", 8 oz.	----	70.00
Stem, 4", 1 oz., Cordial	----	250.00
Stem, 4⅞", 3 oz.	----	150.00
Stem, 5½", 7 oz., Sherbet/ Champagne	----	95.00
Stem, 7½", 11 oz.	----	165.00
Sugar	35.00	18.00
Tray, 11", 2-Handled Cake	65.00	45.00
Tumbler, 5", 6 oz., Ftd. Juice	----	95.00
Tumbler, 6", 10 oz., Water	75.00	33.00
Tumbler, 6⅛", 12½ oz., Iced Tea	----	150.00
Tray, 11", Center-Handled Sandwich	195.00	210.00
Vase, 12"	350.00	350.00

KING'S CROWN, THUMBPRINT
LINE No. 4016 U.S. GLASS (TIFFIN) COMPANY,
Late 1800s – 1960s; INDIANA GLASS COMPANY, 1970s

Ruby Flashed

Ashtray, 5¼", Square	28.00
Bowl, 4", Finger	18.00
Bowl, 4", Mayonnaise	50.00
Bowl 5¾"	20.00
Bowl, 6", Diameter, Ftd., Wedding or Candy	55.00
Bowl, 8¾", 2-Hdld., Crimped Bon Bon	85.00
Bowl, 9¼", Salad	90.00
Bowl, 10½", Ftd., Wedding or Candy, w/Cover	165.00
Bowl, 11½", 4½" High, Crimped	125.00
Bowl, 11¼" Cone	85.00
Bowl, 12½", Center Edge, 3" High	95.00
Bowl, 12½", Flower Floater	80.00
Bowl, Crimped, Ftd.	85.00
Bowl, Flared, Ftd.	85.00
Bowl, Straight Edge	80.00
Cake Salver, 12½", Ftd.	85.00
Candleholder, Sherbet Type	30.00
Candleholder, 2-Lite, 5½"	95.00
Candy Box, 6", Flat, w/Cover	60.00
Cheese Stand	28.00
Compote, 7¼", 9¾" Diameter	50.00
Compote, 7½", 12" Diameter, Ftd., Crimped	95.00
Compote, Small, Flat	25.00
Creamer	25.00
Cup	8.00
Lazy Susan, 24", 8½" High, w/Ball Bearing Spinner	295.00
Mayonnaise, 3 Pc. Set	75.00

Ruby Flashed

Pitcher	195.00
Plate, 5", Bread/Butter	8.00
Plate, 7⅜", Mayonnaise Liner	12.50
Plate, 7⅜", Salad	12.00
Plate, 9¾", Snack w/Indent	15.00
Plate, 10", Dinner	42.00
Plate, 14½", Torte	85.00
Plate, 24", Party	185.00
Plate, 24", Party Server (w/Punch Ft.)	295.00
Punch Bowl Foot	150.00
Punch Bowl, 2 Styles	450.00
Punch Cup	15.00
Punch Set, 15 Pc. w/Foot	895.00
Punch Set, 15 Pc. w/Plate	850.00
Relish, 14", 5 Part	110.00
Saucer	8.00
Stem, 2 oz., Wine	7.50
Stem, 2¼ oz., Cocktail	12.50
Stem, 4 oz., Claret	13.00
Stem, 4 oz., Oyster Cocktail	14.00
Stem, 5½ oz., Sundae or Sherbet	10.00
Stem, 9 oz., Water Goblet	12.00
Sugar	25.00
Tumbler, 4 oz., Juice, Ftd.	12.00
Tumbler, 4½ oz., Juice	14.00
Tumbler, 8½ oz., Water	13.00
Tumbler, 11 oz., Iced Tea	16.00
Tumbler, 12 oz., Iced Tea, Ftd.	20.00
Vase, 9", Bud	95.00
Vase, 12¼", Bud	125.00

LACED EDGE, "KATY BLUE"
(blue with opalescent edge; green with opalescent edge)
IMPERIAL GLASS COMPANY, Early 1930s

	Blue or Green		Blue or Green
Bowl, 4½", Fruit	30.00	Plate, 6½", Bread & Butter	18.00
Bowl, 5"	37.50	Plate, 8", Salad	35.00
Bowl, 7", Soup	85.00	Plate, 10", Dinner	85.00
Bowl, 9", Vegetable	100.00	Plate, 12", Luncheon	
Bowl, 11", Divided Oval	115.00	(per catalog description)	80.00
Bowl, 11", Oval	150.00	Platter, 13"	175.00
Candlestick, Double, Pr.	175.00	Saucer	15.00
Cup	35.00	Sugar	40.00
Creamer	40.00	Tidbit, w/8" & 10" Plates	110.00
Mayonnaise, Three-Piece	135.00	Tumbler, 9 oz.	55.00

LAKE COMO

(white with blue decoration)
ANCHOR HOCKING GLASS COMPANY, 1934 – 1937

Bowl, 6", Cereal	28.00	Plate, Salad, 7¼"	20.00
Bowl, Flat Soup	105.00	Plate, Dinner, 9¼"	35.00
Bowl, Vegetable, 9¾"	65.00	Platter, 11"	75.00
Creamer, Footed	32.50	Salt & Pepper, Pr.	45.00
Cup, Regular	30.00	Saucer	12.00
Cup, St. Denis	30.00	Sugar, Footed	32.50

LAUREL

(French ivory, jade green, white opal, and poudre blue)
McKEE GLASS COMPANY, 1930s

	Ivory	Jade
Bowl, 4¾" Berry	9.00	15.00
Bowl, 6", Cereal	12.00	25.00
Bowl, 6", Three Legs	15.00	25.00
Bowl, 9", Large Berry	28.00	40.00
Bowl, 9¾", Oval Vegetable	28.00	50.00
Bowl, 10½", Three Legs	40.00	60.00
Bowl, 11"	40.00	60.00
Candlesticks, 4", Pr.	40.00	60.00
Cheese Dish & Cover	58.00	90.00
Creamer, Short	10.00	20.00
Creamer, Tall	15.00	24.00
Cup	9.00	15.00
Plate, 6", Sherbet	10.00	16.00
Plate, 7½", Salad	10.00	20.00
Plate, 9⅛", Dinner	15.00	25.00
Plate, 9⅛", Grill	15.00	25.00
Platter, 10¾", Oval	30.00	45.00

	Ivory	Jade
Salt & Pepper	50.00	80.00
Saucer	3.50	5.00
Sherbet	12.00	20.00
Sugar, Short	10.00	20.00
Sugar, Tall	15.00	24.00
Tumbler, 4½", 9 oz., Flat	40.00	60.00
Tumbler, 5", 12 oz., Flat	55.00	----

CHILDREN'S LAUREL TEA SET

	Ivory	Jade
Creamer	25.00	50.00
Cup	20.00	35.00
Plate	10.00	16.00
Saucer	8.00	10.00
Sugar	25.00	50.00
14-Piece Set	205.00	345.00

LINCOLN INN

(amethyst, cobalt, black, red, green, pink, crystal, jade, opaque, green)
FENTON GLASS COMPANY, Late 1920s

	Blue, Red	Other Colors		Blue, Red	Other Colors
Ashtray	17.50	12.00	Nut Dish, Footed	25.00	12.00
Bonbon, Handled, Square	15.00	12.00	Pitcher, 7¼", 46 oz.	800.00	700.00
Bonbon, Handled, Oval	16.00	12.00	Plate, 6"	7.50	4.50
			Plate, 8"	12.50	7.50
Bowl, 5", Fruit	12.00	9.00	Plate, 9¼"	35.00	12.50
Bowl, 6", Cereal	14.00	9.00	Plate, 12"	40.00	17.50
Bowl, 6", Crimped	15.00	9.00	Salt & Pepper, Pr	275.00	175.00
Bowl, Handled, Olive	15.00	10.00	Sandwich Server, Center Handled	175.00	100.00
Bowl, Finger	20.00	14.00	Saucer	5.00	3.50
Bowl, 9¼", Footed	75.00	30.00	Sherbet, 4¾"	20.00	12.50
Bowl, 10½", Footed	75.00	35.00	Sugar	20.00	15.00
Candy Dish, Footed, Oval	45.00	20.00	Tumbler, Flat Juice, 4 oz.	30.00	10.00
Comport	30.00	15.00	Tumbler, 5 oz., Footed	30.00	12.00
Creamer	22.50	15.00	Tumbler, 9 oz., Footed	30.00	14.00
Cup	20.00	10.00	Tumbler, 12 oz., Footed	45.00	20.00
Goblet, Water	27.00	17.50	Vase, 9¾"	150.00	125.00
Goblet, Wine	30.00	17.50	Vase, 12", Footed	195.00	100.00

LORAIN, "BASKET," "NO. 615"
(green, yellow, crystal)
INDIANA GLASS COMPANY, 1929 – 1932

	Green	Yellow
Bowl, 6", Cereal	48.00	68.00
Bowl, 7¼", Salad	48.00	68.00
Bowl, 8", Deep Berry	110.00	175.00
Bowl, 9¾", Oval Vegetable	50.00	65.00
Creamer, Footed	20.00	28.00
Cup	11.00	15.00
Plate, 5½", Sherbet	10.00	12.50
Plate, 7¾", Salad	10.00	15.00
Plate, 8⅜", Luncheon	20.00	30.00
Plate, 10¼", Dinner	48.00	65.00
Platter, 11½"	33.00	48.00
Relish, 8", Four-Part	20.00	38.00
Saucer	4.50	6.00
Sherbet, Footed	25.00	35.00
Sugar, Footed	20.00	28.00
Tumbler, 4¾", 9 oz., Footed	25.00	35.00

MADRID

(See Reproduction Section, Pages 176 – 177)
(green, pink, amber, crystal, "Madonna" blue)
FEDERAL GLASS COMPANY, 1932 – 1939

	Amber	Green
Ashtray, 6", Square	225.00	195.00
Bowl, 4¾", Cream Soup..	18.00	----
Bowl, 5", Sauce..............	7.00	7.00
Bowl, 7", Soup................	15.00	16.00
Bowl, 8", Salad...............	14.00	17.50
Bowl, 9⅜", Large Berry ...	20.00	----
Bowl, 9½", Deep Salad ...	30.00	----
Bowl, 10", Oval Vegetable..	15.00	22.00
Bowl, 11", Low Console..	15.00	----
Butter Dish & Cover.......	70.00	90.00
Candlesticks, 2¼", Pr.....	22.00	----
Cookie Jar & Cover	45.00	----
Creamer, Footed.............	8.00	11.00
Cup	6.00	8.50
Gravy Boat & Platter........	2,000.00	----
Hot Dish Coaster	50.00	50.00
Hot Dish Coaster w/Indent	55.00	55.00
Jam Dish, 7"	25.00	20.00
Jello Mold, 2⅛" High	15.00	----
Pitcher, 5½", Juice, 36 oz.	40.00	----
Pitcher, 8", Square, 60 oz.	50.00	145.00
Pitcher, 8½", 8 oz.	60.00	200.00
Pitcher, 8½", 80 oz., Ice Lip..........................	60.00	225.00

	Amber	Green
Plate, 6", Sherbet	4.00	4.00
Plate, 7½", Salad.............	10.00	9.00
Plate, 8⅞", Luncheon	8.00	9.00
Plate, 10½", Dinner..........	55.00	40.00
Plate, 10½", Grill..............	9.50	15.00
Plate, 10¼", Relish	15.00	16.00
Plate, 11½", Cake, Round.........................	20.00	----
Platter, 11½", Oval	15.00	16.00
Salt/Pepper, 3½", Footed......................	135.00	110.00
Salt/Pepper, 3½", Flat	45.00	65.00
Saucer.............................	3.00	5.00
Sherbet, Two Styles	7.50	11.00
Sugar	7.00	12.00
Sugar Cover.....................	50.00	60.00
Tumbler, 3⅞", 5 oz.	14.00	32.00
Tumbler, 4¼", 9 oz.	15.00	21.00
Tumbler, 5½", 12 oz., Two Styles..................	22.00	30.00
Tumbler, 4", 5 oz., Footed..	28.00	40.00
Tumbler, 5½", 10 oz., Footed	30.00	40.00
Wooden Lazy Susan, 7 Hot Dish Coasters....	895.00	----

MANHATTAN, "HORIZONTAL RIBBED"
(pink, crystal, green)
ANCHOR HOCKING GLASS COMPANY, 1939 – 1941

	Crystal	Pink
Ashtray, 4", Round	12.00	----
Ashtray, 4½", Square	18.00	----
Bowl, 4½", Sauce w/handles..	9.00	----
Bowl, 5⅜", Berry w/Handles	18.00	20.00
Bowl, 5¼", Cereal	65.00	125.00
Bowl, 7½", Large Berry	15.00	----
Bowl, 8", Closed Handles ..	25.00	28.00
Bowl, 9", Salad	28.00	----
Bowl, 9½", Fruit (Open Handle)	35.00	40.00
Candlesticks, 4½" (Square) Pr.	22.00	----
Candy Dish, Three Legs	----	15.00
Coaster, 3½"	16.00	----
Compote, 5¾"	33.00	38.00
Creamer, Oval	12.00	15.00
Cup	18.00	250.00

	Crystal	Pink
Relish Tray, 14", Four-Part	30.00	----
Relish Tray, 14", Five-Part	30.00	18.00
Relish Tray Insert	5.50	6.00
Pitcher, 42 oz.	35.00	----
Pitcher, 80 oz., Tilted	50.00	75.00
Plate, 6", Sherbet	8.00	75.00
Plate, 8½", Salad	20.00	----
Plate, 10¼", Dinner	25.00	195.00
Plate, 14", Sandwich	25.00	----
Salt/Pepper, 2" (Square), Pr.	30.00	50.00
Saucer (Same as 6" Plate)..	7.00	75.00
Sherbet	12.00	18.00
Sugar, Oval	12.00	15.00
Tumbler, 10 oz., Footed	20.00	22.00
Vase, 8"	25.00	----
Wine, 3½"	5.50	----

MAYFAIR FEDERAL
(crystal, amber, green)
FEDERAL GLASS COMPANY, 1934

	Amber	Green
Bowl, 5", Sauce	9.00	12.00
Bowl, 5", Cream Soup	20.00	22.00
Bowl, 6", Cereal	18.00	20.00
Bowl, 10", Oval Vegetable	30.00	35.00
Creamer, Footed	13.00	16.00
Cup	9.00	10.00

	Amber	Green
Plate, 6¾", Salad	7.00	9.00
Plate, 9½", Dinner	14.00	14.00
Plate, 9½", Grill	14.00	14.00
Platter, 12", Oval	30.00	35.00
Saucer	4.00	4.00
Sugar, Footed	13.00	16.00
Tumbler, 4½", 9 oz.	30.00	35.00

MAYFAIR, "OPEN ROSE"

(See Reproduction Section, Pages 178 – 180)
(pink, green, blue, yellow, crystal, satinized pink or blue)
HOCKING GLASS COMPANY, 1931 – 1937

	Pink	Blue
Bowl, 5", Cream Soup ...	55.00	----
Bowl, 5½", Cereal	30.00	60.00
Bowl, 7", Vegetable........	30.00	60.00
Bowl, 9", 3⅛" High, Three Leg Console	5,500.00	----
Bowl, 9½", Oval Vegetable..................	35.00	80.00
Bowl, 10", Vegetable......	35.00	80.00
Bowl, 10", Same Covered	135.00	150.00
Bowl, 11¾", Low Flat.....	60.00	75.00
Bowl, 12", Deep Scalloped Fruit..........	65.00	100.00
Butter Dish & Cover or 7" Covered Vegetable	75.00	325.00
Cake Plate, Footed	35.00	75.00
Candy Dish & Cover.......	55.00	315.00
Celery Dish, 10"	50.00	75.00
Celery Dish, 10", Divided.......................	265.00	75.00
Cookie Jar & Lid.............	55.00	295.00
Creamer, Footed	35.00	85.00

	Pink	Blue
Cup................................	20.00	55.00
Decanter & Stopper, 32 oz.	215.00	----
Goblet, 4" Cocktail, 3 oz.	100.00	----
Goblet, 4½", Wine, 3 oz.	110.00	----
Goblet, 5¾", Water, 9 oz	75.00	----
Goblet, 7¼", Thin, 9 oz.	250.00	225.00
Pitcher, 6", 37 oz.	65.00	165.00
Pitcher, 8", 60 oz.	75.00	195.00
Pitcher, 8½", 80 oz.	125.00	225.00
Plate, 5¾" (often substituted as saucer)	15.00	25.00
Plate, 6½", Round Sherbet	15.00	----
Plate, 6½", Round, Off Center Indent.............	25.00	28.00
Plate, 8½", Luncheon.....	33.00	55.00
Plate, 9½", Dinner..........	60.00	80.00
Plate, 9½", Grill	50.00	60.00

MAYFAIR, "OPEN ROSE"

	Pink	Blue
Plate, 12", Cake		
w/Handles	50.00	75.00
Platter, 12", Oval, Open		
Handles	33.00	75.00
Relish, 8⅜", Four-Part	33.00	75.00
Relish, 8⅜"		
Non-Partitioned	235.00	----
Salt & Pepper,		
Flat, Pr.	65.00	325.00
Salt & Pepper,		
Footed, Pr.	9,500.00	----
Sandwich Server/		
Center Handle	50.00	82.50
Saucer (Cup Ring)	35.00	----
Saucer (See 5¾" Plate)		
Sherbet, 2¼", Flat	195.00	145.00
Sherbet, 3", Footed	17.50	----
Sherbet, 4¾", Footed	90.00	80.00

	Pink	Blue
Sugar, Footed	35.00	85.00
Sugar Lid	1,650.00	----
Tumbler, 3½", Juice,		
5 oz.	45.00	125.00
Tumbler, 4¼", Water,		
9 oz.	33.00	110.00
Tumbler, 4¾", Water,		
11 oz.	225.00	150.00
Tumbler, 5¼", 13½ oz.,		
Iced Tea	65.00	275.00
Tumbler, 3¼", Juice,		
3 oz., Footed	85.00	----
Tumbler, 5¼", 10 oz.,		
Footed	45.00	150.00
Tumbler, 6½", Iced Tea,		
15 oz., Footed	48.00	295.00
Vase (Sweet Pea)	150.00	125.00
Whiskey, 2¼", 1½ oz.	70.00	----

MISS AMERICA
(See Reproduction Section, Pages 181 – 182)
(pink, green, crystal, red)
HOCKING GLASS COMPANY, 1933 – 1937

	Crystal	Pink		Crystal	Pink
Bowl, 6¼", Berry	11.00	28.00	Plate, 5¾", Sherbet	7.00	12.00
Bowl, 8", Curved in at top	40.00	90.00	Plate, 8½", Salad	8.00	27.00
Bowl, 8¾", Straight, Deep Fruit	35.00	80.00	Plate, 10¼", Dinner	16.00	36.00
			Plate, 10¼", Grill	11.00	27.00
Bowl, 10", Oval Vegetable	15.00	40.00	Platter, 12", Oval	15.00	40.00
Butter Dish & Cover	225.00	625.00	Relish, 8¾", Four-Part	11.00	27.00
Cake Plate, 12", Footed	26.00	60.00	Relish, 11¾", Round, Divided	25.00	5,500.00
Candy Jar & Cover, 11½"	65.00	165.00	Salt & Pepper, Pr.	33.00	65.00
Celery Dish, 10½", Oblong	16.00	40.00	Saucer	4.00	7.00
Coaster, 5¾"	16.00	35.00	Sherbet	9.00	16.00
Compote, 5"	16.00	30.00	Sugar	9.00	22.00
Creamer, Footed	11.00	22.00	Tumbler, 4", Juice, 5 oz.	17.00	55.00
Cup	11.00	27.00	Tumbler, 4½", Water, 10 oz.	16.00	36.00
Goblet, 3¾", Wine, 3 oz.	24.00	110.00			
Goblet, 4¾", Juice, 5 oz.	30.00	100.00	Tumbler, 5¾", Iced Tea, 14 oz.	30.00	95.00
Goblet, 5½", Water, 10 oz.	22.00	52.00			
Pitcher, 8", 65 oz.	50.00	135.00			
Pitcher, 8½", 65 oz., w/Ice Lip	70.00	225.00			

MODERNTONE, "WEDDING BAND"
(blue, amethyst, platonite fired-on colors)
HAZEL ATLAS GLASS COMPANY, 1934 – 1942

	Cobalt	Amethyst
Ashtray, 7¾", Match Holder in Center	165.00	----
Bowl, 4¾", Cream Soup	25.00	22.00
Bowl, 5", Berry	28.00	25.00
Bowl, 5", Cream Soup, Ruffled	65.00	33.00
Bowl, 6½", Cereal	75.00	75.00
Bowl, 7½", Soup	150.00	100.00
Bowl, 8¾", Large Berry	50.00	40.00
Butter Dish w/Metal Cover	100.00	----
Cheese Dish, 7" w/Metal Lid	495.00	----
Creamer	12.00	11.00
Cup	12.00	12.00
Cup (no handle), Custard	22.00	15.00

	Cobalt	Amethyst
Plate, 5¾", Sherbet	6.50	5.00
Plate, 6¾", Salad	12.50	10.00
Plate, 7¾", Luncheon	12.50	9.00
Plate, 8⅞", Dinner	21.00	13.00
Plate, 10½", Sandwich	60.00	40.00
Platter, 11", Oval	50.00	37.50
Platter, 12", Oval	80.00	50.00
Salt & Pepper, Pr.	43.00	35.00
Saucer	5.00	4.00
Sherbet	14.00	12.00
Sugar	12.00	11.00
Sugar Lid in Metal	37.50	----
Tumbler, 5 oz.	65.00	35.00
Tumbler, 9 oz.	38.00	30.00
Tumbler, 12 oz.	125.00	90.00
Whiskey, 1½ oz.	45.00	----

MODERNTONE PLATONITE
HAZEL ATLAS GLASS COMPANY, 1940 – Early 1950s

	Pastel Colors	Deco Red/Blue Willow		Pastel Colors	Deco Red/Blue Willow
Bowl, 4¾", Cream Soup	6.50	20.00	Plate, 6¾", Sherbet....	4.50	9.00
Bowl, 5", Berry, w/Rim.	5.00	12.50	Plate, 8⅞", Dinner	6.50	25.00
Bowl, 5", Berry, wo/Rim	6.00	----	Plate, 10½", Sandwich..	17.00	----
Bowl, 5", Deep Cereal, w/White	7.50	----	Platter, 11", Oval	----	35.00
Bowl, 5", Deep Cereal, wo/White	9.00	----	Platter, 12", Oval	**15.00	45.00
Bowl, 8", w/Rim	*14.00	35.00	Salt and Pepper, Pr....	16.00	----
Bowl, 8", wo/Rim	*20.00	----	Saucer	1.00	5.00
Bowl, 8¾", Large Berry..	----	35.00	Sherbet........................	4.50	15.00
Creamer......................	5.00	22.00	Sugar...........................	5.00	22.00
Cup............................	3.50	20.00	Tumbler, 9 oz.	9.00	----

*Pink $8.50
* *Yellow $8.00

MOONDROPS

(amber, pink, green, cobalt blue, ice blue, red, amethyst, crystal, dark green, light green, jadite, smoke, black)
NEW MARTINSVILLE, 1932 – 1940s

	Red, Blue	Others
Ashtray	32.00	17.00
Bowl, 4¼", Cream Soup	95.00	35.00
Bowl, 5¼", Berry	25.00	12.00
Bowl, 6¾", Soup	90.00	40.00
Bowl, 7½", Pickle	35.00	20.00
Bowl, 8⅜", Footed, Concave Top	45.00	25.00
Bowl, 8½", Three-Footed, Divided Relish	40.00	20.00
Bowl, 9½", Three-Legged, Ruffled	70.00	----
Bowl, 9¾", Oval Vegetable	75.00	45.00
Bowl, 9¾", Covered Casserole	195.00	100.00
Bowl, 9¾", Two Handled, Oval	52.50	37.50
Bowl, 11½", Celery, Boat Shaped	35.00	25.00
Bowl, 12", Three-Footed, Round Casserole	85.00	35.00

	Red, Blue	Others
Bowl, 13", Console w/"Wings"	120.00	50.00
Butter Dish & Cover	450.00	275.00
Candles, 2", Ruffled, Pr.	45.00	25.00
Candles, 4½", Sherbet Style, Pr.	30.00	22.00
Candlesticks, 5" "Wings," Pr.	110.00	60.00
Candlesticks, 5¼", Triple Light, Pr.	150.00	95.00
Candlesticks, 8½", Metal Stem, Pr.	45.00	30.00
Candy Dish, 8", Ruffled	40.00	20.00
Cocktail Shaker with or w/o Handle, Metal Top	60.00	35.00
Compote, 4"	27.50	18.00
Compote, 11½"	95.00	55.00
Creamer, 2¾", Miniature	18.00	11.00
Creamer, 3¾", Regular	16.00	10.00
Cup	18.00	10.00
Decanter, Small, 7¾"	70.00	40.00

MOONDROPS ⊂===========================⊃

	Red, Blue	Others
Decanter, Medium, 8½"	75.00	45.00
Decanter, Large, 11¼"	110.00	55.00
Decanter, "Rocket," 10¼"	450.00	395.00
Goblet, 2⅞", ¾ oz., Liquor	40.00	28.00
Goblet, 4", Wine, 4 oz.	25.00	15.00
Goblet, 4¼", "Rocket" Wine	60.00	35.00
Goblet, 4¾", 5 oz.	25.00	15.00
Goblet, 5⅛", 3 oz., Wine, Metal Stem	18.00	11.00
Goblet, 5½", 4 oz., Wine, Metal Stem	20.00	11.00
Goblet, 6¼", Water, 9 oz., Metal Stem	27.50	16.00
Mug, 5⅛", 12 oz.	45.00	27.50
Perfume Bottle, "Rocket"	250.00	195.00
Pitcher, Small, 6⅞", 22 oz.	165.00	90.00
Pitcher, Medium, 8⅛", 32 oz.	185.00	115.00
Pitcher, Large w/Lip, 8", 50 oz.	195.00	115.00
Pitcher, Large, No Lip, 8⅛", 53 oz.	185.00	125.00
Plate, 5⅞", Bread & Butter	11.00	8.00
Plate, 6⅛", Sherbet	8.00	5.00
Plate, 6", Round, Off-Center Indent for Sherbet	12.00	9.00
Plate, 7⅛", Salad	14.00	10.00

	Red, Blue	Others
Plate, 8½", Luncheon	15.00	12.00
Plate, 9½", Dinner	30.00	20.00
Plate, 14", Round Sandwich	45.00	20.00
Plate, 14", Two-Handled Sandwich	60.00	25.00
Platter, 12", Oval	45.00	25.00
Saucer	6.00	5.00
Sherbet, 2⅝"	16.00	11.00
Sherbet, 4½"	30.00	16.00
Sugar, 2¾"	15.00	10.00
Sugar, 4"	16.00	11.00
Tumbler, 2¾", Shot, 2 oz.	20.00	10.00
Tumbler, 2¾", Handled Shot, 2 oz.	16.00	11.00
Tumbler, 3¾", Juice, 3 oz., Footed	16.00	11.00
Tumbler, 3⅝", 5 oz.	15.00	10.00
Tumbler, 4⅜", 7 oz.	16.00	10.00
Tumbler, 4⅜", 8 oz.	20.00	11.00
Tumbler, 4⅞", Handled, 9 oz.	30.00	16.00
Tumbler, 4⅞", 9 oz.	20.00	15.00
Tumbler, 5⅛", 12 oz.	32.00	15.00
Tray, 7½" for Miniature Sugar/Creamer	40.00	20.00
Vase, 7¾", Flat, Ruffled Top	75.00	60.00
Vase, 8½", "Rocket" bud	275.00	185.00
Vase, 9¼", "Rocket" Style	250.00	150.00

MOONSTONE

(crystal with opalescent hobnails)
ANCHOR HOCKING GLASS COMPANY, 1941 – 1946

	Opalescent
Bowl, 5½", Berry	20.00
Bowl, 5½", Crimped Dessert	9.50
Bowl, 6½", Crimped, Handled	10.00
Bowl, 7¾", Flat	12.00
Bowl, 7¾", Divided Relish	12.00
Bowl, 9½", Crimped	25.00
Bowl, Cloverleaf	13.00
Candleholder, Pr.	18.00
Candy Jar & Cover, 6"	28.00
Cigarette Jar & Cover	23.00
Creamer	9.00

	Opalescent
Cup	8.00
Goblet, 10 oz.	18.00
Heart Bonbon, One Handle	14.00
Plate, 6¼", Sherbet	6.00
Plate, 8", Luncheon	15.00
Plate, 10", Sandwich	27.50
Puff Box & Cover, 4¾", Round	25.00
Saucer (same as Sherbet Plate)	6.00
Sherbet, Footed	7.00
Sugar, Footed	9.00
Vase, 5½", Bud	13.00

MOROCCAN AMETHYST
(amethyst)
HAZEL WARE, DIVISION OF CONTINENTAL CAN, 1960s

	Amethyst		Amethyst
Ashtray, 3¼", Triangular	5.50	Goblet, 4¼", 7½ oz., Sherbet	7.50
Ashtray, 3¼", Round	5.50	Goblet, 4⅜", 5½ oz., Juice	9.00
Ashtray, 6⅝", Triangular	9.50	Goblet, 5½", 9 oz., Water	10.00
Ashtray, 8", Square	13.00	Ice Bucket, 6"	37.50
Bowl, 4¾", Fruit, Octagonal	7.50	Plate, 5¾"	4.50
Bowl, 5¾", Deep, Square	10.00	Plate, 7¼", Salad	7.00
Bowl, 6", Round	11.00	Plate, 9⅜", Dinner	9.00
Bowl, 7¾", Oval	16.00	Plate, 10" Fan-shaped,	
Bowl, 7¾", Rectangular	14.00	Snack w/Cup Rest	8.00
Bowl, 7¾", Rectangular, w/Metal		Plate, 12" Sandwich w/Metal	
Handle	18.00	Handle	17.50
Bowl, 10¾"	30.00	Saucer	1.00
Candy w/Lid, Short	35.00	Tumbler, 2½", Juice, 4 oz.	8.50
Candy w/Lid, Tall	35.00	Tumbler, 3¼", Old Fashion, 8 oz.	14.00
Chip and dip, 10¾" & 5¾",		Tumbler, Water, 9 oz.	10.00
Bowls in Metal Holder	40.00	Tumbler, 4¼", Water, Crinkled	
Cocktail w/Stirrer, 6¼", 16 oz., w/Lip	32.00	Bottom, 11 oz.	12.00
Cocktail Shaker, w/Lid	30.00	Tumbler, 4⅝", Water, 11 oz.	12.00
Cup	5.00	Tumbler, 6½", Iced Tea, 16 oz.	16.00
Goblet, 4", 4½ oz., Wine	10.00	Vase, 8½", Ruffled	37.50

MT. PLEASANT, "DOUBLE SHIELD"
(black amethyst, amethyst, cobalt blue, green, pink)
L.E. SMITH COMPANY, 1920s – 1934

	Black Amethyst, Cobalt		Black Amethyst, Cobalt
Bonbon, Rolled up Handles, 7"......	23.00	Leaf, 8"	18.00
Bowl, 4" Opening Rose	26.00	Leaf, 11¼"	30.00
Bowl, 4", Square Fruit, Footed	20.00	Mayonnaise, 5½", 3-Footed	30.00
Bowl, 6", Two-Handled, Square	18.00	Mint, 6", Center Handle	25.00
Bowl, 7", Three-Footed, Rolled Out Edge	25.00	Plate, 7", Two-Handled, Scalloped ..	15.00
Bowl, 8", Scalloped, Two-Handled ..	35.00	Plate, 8", Scalloped or Square	15.00
Bowl, 8", Square, Two-Handled	35.00	Plate, 8", Two-Handled	18.00
Bowl, 9", Scalloped, 1¾" Deep, Footed	35.00	Plate, 8¼" Sq. w/Indent for Cup	16.00
Bowl, 9¼", Square Fruit, Footed....	33.00	Plate, 9", Grill	20.00
Bowl, 10", Scalloped Fruit	42.00	Plate, 10½", Cake, Two-Handled ...	38.00
Bowl, 10", Two-Handled, Turned Up Edge	35.00	Plate, 12", Two-Handled	33.00
Candlesticks, Single, Pr	30.00	Salt & Pepper, Two Styles	45.00
Candlesticks, Double, Pr.	45.00	Sandwich Server, Center Handled .	40.00
Creamer	20.00	Saucer	5.00
Cup (Waffle-like Crystal, $4.50)		Sherbet	18.00
Cup	14.00	Sugar	20.00
		Tumbler, Footed	25.00
		Vase, 7¼"	32.00

NEW CENTURY, and incorrectly, "LYDIA RAY"
(pink, green, crystal, amethyst, cobalt)
HAZEL ATLAS GLASS COMPANY, 1930 – 1935

	Green		Green
Ashtray/Coaster, 5⅜"	28.00	Plate, 8½", Salad	13.00
Bowl, 4½", Berry	25.00	Plate, 10", Dinner	20.00
Bowl, 4¾", Cream Soup	20.00	Plate, 10", Grill	15.00
Bowl, 8", Large Berry	25.00	Platter, 11", Oval	22.00
Bowl, 9", Covered Casserole	75.00	Salt & Pepper, Pr.	35.00
Butter Dish & Cover	60.00	Saucer	3.00
Cup	6.50	Sherbet, 3"	10.00
Creamer	12.00	Sugar	10.00
Decanter & Stopper	65.00	Sugar Cover	18.00
Goblet, Wine, 2½ oz.	30.00	Tumbler, 3½", 5 oz.	15.00
Goblet, Cocktail, 3¼ oz.	30.00	Tumbler, 4¼", 9 oz.	20.00
Pitcher, 7¾", 60 oz., with or without Ice Lip	35.00	Tumbler, 5", 10 oz.	20.00
Pitcher, 8", 80 oz., with or without Ice Lip	40.00	Tumbler, 5¼", 12 oz.	30.00
Plate, 6", Sherbet	5.00	Tumbler, 4", 5 oz., Footed	20.00
Plate, 7⅛", Breakfast	10.00	Tumbler, 4⅞", 9 oz., Footed	22.00
		Whiskey, 2½", 1½ oz.	20.00

NEWPORT, "HAIRPIN"
(cobalt blue, amethyst, "Platonite" white and fired-on colors)
HAZEL ATLAS GLASS COMPANY, 1936 – 1940

	Cobalt	Fired-on Colors		Cobalt	Fired-on Colors
Bowl, 4¼", Berry	22.00	5.50	Plate, 8¹³⁄₁₆", Dinner	30.00	----
Bowl, 4¾", Cream Soup	22.00	8.50	Plate, 11½", Sandwich	45.00	14.00
Bowl, 5¼", Cereal	40.00	----	Platter, 11¾", Oval	48.00	18.00
Bowl, 8¼", Large Berry	42.50	14.00	Salt & Pepper	50.00	22.50
Cup	14.00	6.00	Saucer	5.00	1.00
Creamer	16.00	7.50	Sherbet	15.00	6.00
Plate, 5⅞", Sherbet	9.00	1.50	Sugar	16.00	7.50
Plate, 8½", Luncheon	16.00	5.00	Tumbler, 4½", 9 oz.	42.00	15.00

NORMANDIE, "BOUQUET AND LATTICE"
(iridescent, amber, pink)
FEDERAL GLASS COMPANY, 1933 – 1940

	Amber	Pink		Amber	Pink
Bowl, 5", Berry	9.00	10.00	Plate, 11", Grill	15.00	25.00
Bowl, 6½", Cereal	28.00	35.00	Platter, 11¾"	22.00	35.00
Bowl, 8½", Large Berry	22.00	35.00	Salt & Pepper, Pr.	50.00	90.00
Bowl, 10", Oval Vegetable	20.00	45.00	Saucer	3.00	4.00
Creamer, Footed	9.00	14.00	Sherbet	7.00	9.00
Cup	7.50	10.00	Sugar	8.00	12.00
Pitcher, 8", 80 oz.	85.00	175.00	Sugar Lid	95.00	195.00
Plate, 6", Sherbet	4.00	6.00	Tumbler, 4", Juice, 5 oz.	35.00	90.00
Plate, 7¾", Salad	9.00	14.00	Tumbler, 4¼", Water, 9 oz.	22.00	55.00
Plate, 9¼", Luncheon	9.00	17.00	Tumbler, 5", Iced Tea,		
Plate, 11", Dinner	33.00	115.00	12 oz	40.00	110.00

NO. 610, "PYRAMID"
(green, pink, yellow, crystal) (black and blue, 1974 – 1975 by Tiara)
INDIANA GLASS COMPANY, 1928 – 1932

	Pink	Yellow
Bowl, 4¾", Berry	20.00	40.00
Bowl, 8½", Master Berry	30.00	60.00
Bowl, 9½", Oval	40.00	65.00
Bowl, 9½", Pickle	35.00	55.00
Creamer	35.00	40.00
Ice Tub	115.00	225.00
Ice Tub/Lid	----	650.00
Pitcher	350.00	495.00

	Pink	Yellow
Relish Tray, Four-Part, Handled	45.00	65.00
Sugar	35.00	40.00
Tray for Creamer & Sugar	30.00	55.00
Tumbler, 8 oz., Footed	45.00	75.00
Tumbler, 11 oz., Footed	55.00	95.00

NO. 612, "HORSESHOE"
(green, yellow, crystal)
INDIANA GLASS COMPANY, 1930 – 1933

	Green	Yellow
Bowl, 4½", Berry	28.00	23.00
Bowl, 6½", Cereal	30.00	35.00
Bowl, 7½", Salad	25.00	25.00
Bowl, 8½", Vegetable	40.00	38.00
Bowl, 9½", Large Berry	45.00	50.00
Bowl, 10½", Oval Vegetable	30.00	33.00
Butter Dish & Cover	800.00	----
Candy in Metal Holder, Motif on Lid Only	185.00	----
Creamer, Footed	18.00	19.00
Cup	12.00	14.00
Pitcher, 8½", 64 oz.	285.00	325.00
Plate, 6", Sherbet	8.00	9.00

	Green	Yellow
Plate, 8⅜", Salad	12.00	12.00
Plate, 9⅜", Luncheon	14.00	16.00
Plate, 10⅜", Grill	110.00	135.00
Plate, 11¼", Sandwich	25.00	25.00
Platter, 10¾", Oval	32.00	32.00
Relish, Three-Part, Footed	25.00	40.00
Saucer	5.00	5.00
Sherbet	16.00	18.00
Sugar, Open	18.00	17.00
Tumbler, 4¼", 9 oz.	170.00	----
Tumbler, 4¾", 12 oz.	170.00	----
Tumbler, 9 oz., Footed	30.00	30.00
Tumbler, 12 oz., Footed	160.00	175.00

NO. 616, "VERNON"
(green, crystal, yellow)
INDIANA GLASS COMPANY, 1930 – 1932

	Green	Yellow		Green	Yellow
Creamer, Footed	28.00	28.00	Saucer	4.00	4.00
Cup	18.00	18.00	Sugar, Footed	25.00	25.00
Plate, 8", Luncheon	10.00	10.00	Tumbler, 5", Footed	40.00	38.00
Plate, 11", Sandwich	25.00	25.00			

NO. 618, "PINEAPPLE & FLORAL"
(crystal, amber, fired-on red)
INDIANA GLASS COMPANY, 1932 – 1937

	Crystal	Amber
Ashtray, 4½"	17.50	----
Bowl, 4¾"	25.00	20.00
Bowl, 6", Cereal	30.00	25.00
Bowl, 7", Salad	2.00	10.00
Bowl, 10", Oval Vegetable	25.00	20.00
Compote, Diamond Shaped	1.00	8.00
Creamer, Diamond Shaped	7.50	10.00
Cream Soup	22.00	22.00
Cup	11.00	10.00
Plate, 6", Sherbet	5.00	6.00
Plate, 8⅜", Salad	8.50	8.50

	Crystal	Amber
Plate, 9⅜", Dinner	17.50	14.00
Plate, 11½", Sandwich	17.50	16.00
Platter, 11", Closed Handles	17.50	18.00
Platter, Relish, 11½", Divided	20.00	----
Saucer	4.00	4.00
Sherbet, Footed	22.00	18.00
Sugar, Diamond Shaped	7.50	10.00
Tumbler, 4¼", 8 oz.	40.00	----
Tumbler, 5", 12 oz.	50.00	----
Vase, Cone Shaped, Large	55.00	----

NO. 622, "PRETZEL"
(crystal, teal)
INDIANA GLASS COMPANY, 1930s

	Crystal		Crystal
Bowl, 4½", Fruit Cup	4.50	Plate, 6", Tab Handled	3.00
Bowl, 7", Olive, Leaf Shaped	5.00	Plate, 8⅜", Salad	6.00
Bowl, 7½", Soup	10.00	Plate, 9⅜", Dinner	10.00
Bowl, 8½", Two-Handled, Pickle	5.50	Plate, 11½", Sandwich	12.00
Bowl, 9⅜", Berry	18.00	Saucer	1.00
Bowl, 10¼", Celery	1.50	Sugar	4.50
Creamer	4.50	Tumbler, Juice, 5 oz.	50.00
Cup	6.00	Tumbler, Water, 9 oz.	45.00
Pitcher, 39 oz.	450.00	Tumbler, 12 oz.	70.00
Plate, 6", Bread & Butter	2.50		

OLD CAFE
(pink, crystal, ruby red)
HOCKING GLASS COMPANY, 1936 – 1938; 1940

	Pink	Red
Bowl, 3¾", Berry	9.00	8.00
Bowl, 5", One or Two Handles	10.00	----
Bowl, 5½", Cereal	28.00	15.00
Bowl, 9", Closed Handles	12.00	16.00
Candy Dish, 8", Low	12.00	16.00
Cup	10.00	9.00
Lamp	75.00	95.00
Olive Dish, 6", Oblong	9.00	----

	Pink	Red
Pitcher 6", 36 oz.	95.00	----
Pitcher, 80 oz.	125.00	----
Plate, 6", Sherbet	3.00	----
Plate, 10", Dinner	60.00	----
Saucer	3.00	----
Sherbet, Low Footed	14.00	14.00
Tumbler, 3", Juice	16.00	16.00
Tumbler, 4", Water	20.00	23.00
Vase, 7¼"	40.00	45.00

OLD COLONY
(pink, crystal)
HOCKING GLASS COMPANY, 1935 – 1938

	Pink		Pink
Bowl, 6⅜", Cereal	28.00	Plate, 7¼", Salad	26.00
Bowl, 7¾", Salad	30.00	Plate, 8¾", Luncheon	25.00
Bowl, 9½", Plain or Ribbed	30.00	Plate, 10½", Dinner	36.00
Bowl, 10½", Three Legs	275.00	Plate, 10½", Grill	25.00
Butter Dish or Bon Bon w/Cover.	70.00	Plate, 13", Four-Part Solid Lace..	65.00
Candlesticks, Pr	325.00	Platter, 12¾"	42.00
Candy Jar & Cover, Ribbed	50.00	Platter, 12¾", Five-Part	42.00
Compote, 7"	30.00	Relish Dish, 7½" Deep,	
Compote & Cover, Footed	50.00	Three-Part	70.00
Cookie Jar & Cover	75.00	Saucer	12.00
Creamer	25.00	Sherbet, Footed	115.00
Cup	28.00	Sugar	25.00
Fish Bowl, 1 gal., 80 oz.		Tumbler, 4½", 9 oz., Flat	22.00
(crystal only)	30.00	Tumbler, 5", 10½ oz., Footed	90.00
Flower Bowl, crystal frog	30.00	Vase, 7"	595.00

OLD ENGLISH, "THREADING"
(green, pink, amber)
INDIANA GLASS COMPANY, Late 1920s

	All Colors		All Colors
Bowl, 4", Berry	20.00	Pitcher w/Cover	135.00
Bowl, 9", Footed Fruit	30.00	Plate, Indent for Compote	22.00
Bowl, 9½", Flat	40.00	Sandwich Server, Center Handle	60.00
Candlesticks, 4", Pr.	40.00	Sherbet, Two Styles	22.00
Candy Jar w/Lid, Footed	55.00	Sugar	18.00
Candy & Lid, Flat	55.00	Sugar Cover	40.00
Compote, 3½" Tall, 7" Across	25.00	Tumbler, 4½", Footed	25.00
Creamer	18.00	Tumbler, 5½", Footed	38.00
Fruit Stand, 11", Footed	40.00	Vase, Fan, 7"	60.00
Goblet, 5¾", 8 oz.	35.00	Vase, 12", Footed	75.00
Pitcher	70.00		

"ORCHID"
(amber, blue, crystal, green, pink, red, yellow, black)
PADEN CITY GLASS COMPANY, Early 1930s

	Red Blue		Red Blue
Bowl, 4⅞" Square	50.00	Comport, 6⅝" Tall, 7" Wide	135.00
Bowl, 8½", 2-Handled	135.00	Creamer	95.00
Bowl, 8¾" Square	125.00	Ice Bucket, 6"	195.00
Bowl, 10", Ftd.	195.00	Mayonnaise, 3 Piece	165.00
Bowl, 11", Square	185.00	Plate, 8½", Square	75.00
Candlesticks, 5¾" Pr.	195.00	Sandwich Server, Center Handled.	125.00
Candy with lid, 6½", Square, Three pt	195.00	Sugar	95.00
Comport, 3¼" Tall, 6¼" Wide	50.00	Vase, 8"	275.00
		Vase, 10"	295.00

OVIDE, incorrectly dubbed "New Century" ⊂⊃
(green, white, black)
HAZEL ATLAS GLASS COMPANY, 1930 – 1935

	Green	Decorated White
Bowl, 4¾", Berry	----	7.00
Bowl, 5½", Cereal	----	13.00
Bowl, 8", Large Berry	----	22.50
Candy Dish & Cover	22.50	40.00
Cocktail, Fruit, Footed	4.00	----
Creamer	4.50	17.50
Cup	3.50	12.50

	Green	Decorated White
Plate, 6", Sherbet	2.00	6.00
Plate, 8", Luncheon	3.00	14.00
Salt & Pepper, Pr.	27.50	24.00
Saucer	2.00	5.00
Sherbet	3.00	14.00
Sugar, Open	4.50	17.50
Tumbler	----	17.00

OYSTER AND PEARL

(pink, crystal, ruby red, white with fired-on pink or green)
ANCHOR HOCKING GLASS, 1938 – 1940

	Pink	Red
Bowl, 5¼", Round or Handled	----	16.00
Bowl, 5¼", Heart Shaped, One Handled	14.00	----
Bowl, 6½" Deep, Handled	18.00	25.00

	Pink	Red
Bowl, 10½", Fruit, Deep	25.00	55.00
Candleholder, 3½", Pr.	35.00	60.00
Plate, 13½", Sandwich	20.00	50.00
Relish Dish, 10¼", Oblong	17.50	----

"PARK AVE."
FEDERAL GLASS COMPANY, 1941 – Early 1970s

	Amber/Crystal		Amber/Crystal
Ashtray, 3½", Square	5.00	Tumbler, 3½", 4½ oz., Juice	5.00
Ashtray, 4½", Square	7.00	Tumbler, 3⅞", 9 oz.	6.00
Bowl, 5", Dessert	5.00	Tumbler, 4¾", 10 oz.	7.00
Bowl, 8½", Vegetable	12.00	Tumbler, 5⅛", 12 oz., Iced Tea	12.00
Tumbler, 2⅛", 1¼ oz., Whiskey	4.00		

"PARROT," SYLVAN
(green, amber, crystal)
FEDERAL GLASS COMPANY, 1931 – 1932

	Green	Amber		Green	Amber
Bowl, 5", Berry	30.00	22.00	Plate, 10½", Grill, Round	32.00	----
Bowl, 7", Soup	50.00	35.00	Plate, 10½", Grill,		
Bowl, 8", Large Berry	95.00	75.00	Square	----	32.00
Bowl, 10", Oval			Platter, 11¼", Oblong	60.00	75.00
Vegetable	65.00	70.00	Salt & Pepper, Pr.	275.00	----
Butter Dish & Cover	395.00	1,300.00	Saucer	15.00	15.00
Creamer, Footed	55.00	75.00	Sherbet, Footed, Cone	25.00	25.00
Cup	42.50	42.50	Sherbet, 4¼" High	1,250.00	----
Hot Plate, 5"	895.00	950.00	Sugar	40.00	50.00
Jam Dish, 7"	----	35.00	Sugar Cover	160.00	500.00
Pitcher, 8½", 80 oz.	2,950.00	----	Tumbler, 4¼", 10 oz.	175.00	125.00
Plate, 5¾", Sherbet	35.00	24.00	Tumbler, 5½", 12 oz.	195.00	150.00
Plate, 7½", Salad	38.00	----	Tumbler, 5¾", Footed,		
Plate, 9", Dinner	55.00	45.00	Heavy	165.00	125.00

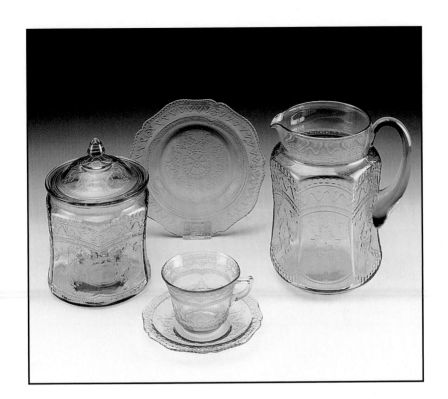

PATRICIAN, "SPOKE"
(pink, green, amber, crystal)
FEDERAL GLASS COMPANY, 1933 – 1937

	Amber	Green
Bowl, 4¾", Cream Soup	18.00	22.00
Bowl, 5", Berry	13.00	12.00
Bowl, 6", Cereal	28.00	30.00
Bowl, 8½", Large Berry	45.00	40.00
Bowl, 10", Oval Vegetable	35.00	35.00
Butter Dish & Cover	90.00	120.00
Cookie Jar & Cover	90.00	595.00
Creamer, Footed	11.00	12.00
Cup	9.00	13.00
Pitcher, 8", 75 oz.	125.00	145.00
Pitcher, 8¼", 75 oz.	----	175.00
Plate, 6", Sherbet	10.00	8.00

	Amber	Green
Plate, 7½", Salad	15.00	14.00
Plate, 9", Luncheon	12.00	14.00
Plate, 10½", Dinner	7.50	45.00
Plate, 10½", Grill	15.00	15.00
Platter, 11½", Oval	30.00	32.00
Salt & Pepper, Pr.	58.00	65.00
Saucer	9.50	9.50
Sherbet	13.00	15.00
Sugar	9.00	10.00
Sugar Cover	60.00	75.00
Tumbler, 4", 5 oz.	33.00	33.00
Tumbler, 4½", 9 oz.	30.00	28.00
Tumbler, 5½", 14 oz.	48.00	50.00
Tumbler, 5½", 8 oz., Footed	55.00	65.00

"PATRICK"
(yellow, pink)
LANCASTER GLASS COMPANY, EARLY 1930s

	Yellow	Pink
Bowl, 9", Fruit, Handled	135.00	175.00
Bowl, 11", Console	135.00	140.00
Candlesticks, Pr.	150.00	195.00
Candy Dish, Three-Footed	175.00	175.00
Cheese & Cracker Set	125.00	150.00
Creamer	37.50	75.00
Cup	35.00	65.00
Goblet, 4", Cocktail	80.00	80.00
Goblet, 4¾", Juice, 6 oz.	75.00	80.00
Goblet, 6", Water, 10 oz.	70.00	90.00
Mayonnaise, Three-Piece	195.00	225.00
Plate, 7", Sherbet	12.00	20.00
Plate, 7½", Salad	20.00	25.00
Plate, 8", Luncheon	27.50	45.00
Saucer	12.00	20.00
Sherbet, 4¾"	60.00	75.00
Sugar	37.50	75.00
Tray, 11", Two-Handled	60.00	75.00
Tray, 11", Center-Handled	110.00	155.00

"PEACOCK REVERSE"

(amber, black, crystal, cobalt blue, green, pink, red, yellow)
PADEN CITY GLASS COMPANY, LINE #412, 1930s

	All Colors
Bowl, 4⅞" Square	42.00
Bowl, 8¾" Square	115.00
Bowl, 8¾" Square with Handles	110.00
Bowl, 11¾" Console	125.00
Candlesticks, 5¾" Square Base, Pr.	150.00
Candy Dish, 6½" Square	175.00
Comport, 3¼" High, 6¼" Wide	75.00
Comport, 4¼" High, 7⅜" Wide	85.00
Creamer, 2¾" Flat	95.00
Cup	90.00

	All Colors
Plate, 5¾" Sherbet	22.50
Plate, 8½" Luncheon	60.00
Plate 10⅜", 2-Handled	100.00
Saucer	25.00
Sherbet, 4⅝" Tall, 3⅝" Diameter	65.00
Sherbet, 4⅞" Tall, 3⅝" Diameter	65.00
Server, Center-Handled	75.00
Sugar, 2¾" Flat	95.00
Tumbler, 4", 10 oz. Flat	85.00
Vase, 10"	225.00

"PEACOCK & WILD ROSE," "NORA BIRD"
(amber, white, cobalt blue, black, green, pink, red)
PADEN CITY GLASS COMPANY, LINE #1300, 1930s

All Colors

Bowl, 8½", Flat	125.00
Bowl, 8½", Fruit, Oval, Ftd.	195.00
Bowl, 8¾", Ftd.	175.00
Bowl, 9½", Center-Handled	165.00
Bowl, 9½", Ftd.	185.00
Bowl, 10½", Center-Handled	125.00
Bowl, 10½", Ftd.	195.00
Bowl, 10½", Fruit	185.00
Bowl, 11", Console	175.00
Bowl, 14", Console	195.00
Candlestick, 5", Pr.	165.00
Candy Dish w/Cover, 6½", 3 Part	195.00
Candy w/Lid, Ftd., 5¼" High	195.00
Candy Dish w/Cover, 7"	250.00
Cheese and Cracker Set	185.00
Comport, 3¼" Tall, 6¼" Wide	125.00
Creamer, 4½", Round Handle	55.00
Creamer, 5", Pointed Handle	55.00
Cup	70.00

All Colors

Ice Bucket, 6"	210.00
Ice Tub, 4¾"	195.00
Ice Tub, 6"	195.00
Mayonnaise and Liner	110.00
Pitcher, 5" High	350.00
Plate, 8"	25.00
Plate, cake, Low Foot	145.00
Relish, 3-Part	110.00
Saucer	15.00
Sugar, 4½", Round Handle	55.00
Sugar, 5", Pointed Handle	55.00
Tumbler, 2¼", 3 oz.	50.00
Tumbler, 3"	55.00
Tumbler, 4"	65.00
Tumbler, 4¾", Ftd.	75.00
Tumbler, 5¼", 10 oz.	75.00
Vase, 8¼" Elliptical	395.00
Vase, 10", Two Styles	265.00
Vase, 12"	325.00

PETALWARE
(pink, crystal, monax, cremax)
MacBETH-EVANS GLASS COMPANY, 1930 – 1940

	Pink	Monax		Pink	Monax
Bowl, 4½", Cream Soup	17.50	12.00	Plate, 6", Sherbet	2.50	2.50
Bowl, 5¾", Cereal	14.00	8.00	Plate, 8", Salad	6.00	5.00
Bowl, 9", Large Berry	25.00	18.00	Plate, 9", Dinner	14.00	13.00
Cup	9.00	5.00	Plate, 11", Salver	15.00	10.00
Creamer, Footed	8.00	6.00	Platter, 13", Oval	25.00	18.00
Lamp Shade (Many Sizes)	----	8.00	Saucer	2.00	2.00
Mustard w/Metal Cover in			Sherbet, Low, Footed	10.00	8.00
Cobalt Blue Only	----	10.00	Sugar, Footed	9.00	6.00

PRIMO, "PANELLED ASTER"
(green, yellow)
U.S. COMPANY, Early 1930s

	Yellow/Green		Yellow/Green
Bowl, 4½"	24.00	Plate, 7½"	12.00
Bowl, 7¾"	35.00	Plate, 10", Dinner	25.00
Cake Plate, 10",		Plate, 10", Grill	16.00
Three-Footed	35.00	Saucer	3.00
Coaster/Ashtray	8.00	Sherbet	14.00
Creamer	12.00	Sugar	12.00
Cup	12.00	Tumbler, 5¾", 9 oz.	30.00

PRINCESS

(green, pink, topaz, apricot, some blue)
HOCKING GLASS COMPANY, 1931 – 1935

	Pink	Green
Ashtray, 4½"	95.00	75.00
Bowl, 4½", Berry	30.00	30.00
Bowl, 5", Cereal or Oatmeal.	40.00	40.00
Bowl, 9", Salad, Octagonal	40.00	42.00
Bowl, 9½", Hat Shaped	50.00	55.00
Bowl, 10", Oval Vegetable	30.00	30.00
Butter Dish & Cover	115.00	100.00
Cake Stand, 10"	35.00	33.00
* Candy Dish & Cover	70.00	65.00
Coaster	85.00	45.00
Cookie Jar & Cover	70.00	60.00
Creamer, Oval	15.00	18.00
Cup	13.00	12.00
Pitcher, 6", 37 oz.	65.00	58.00
Pitcher, 7⅜", 24 oz., Footed	500.00	550.00
Pitcher, 8", 60 oz.	60.00	58.00
Plate, 5½", Sherbet	10.00	10.00
Plate, 8", Salad	16.00	15.00
Plate, 9½", Dinner	27.00	30.00
Plate, 9½", Grill	16.00	15.00
Plate, 10½", Grill, Closed Handles	12.00	14.00

*Recently Reproduced – BEWARE!

	Pink	Green
Plate, 10¼", Sandwich, Handled	30.00	20.00
Platter, 12", Closed Handles	27.00	28.00
Relish, 7½", Divided	30.00	28.00
Relish, 7½", Plain	200.00	200.00
Salt & Pepper, 4½", Pr.	60.00	55.00
Saucer (Same as Sherbet Plate)	10.00	10.00
Sherbet, Footed	25.00	25.00
Sugar	12.00	10.00
Sugar Cover	23.00	25.00
Tumbler, 3", Juice, 5 oz.	33.00	33.00
Tumbler, 4", Water, 9 oz.	28.00	28.00
Tumbler, 5¼", Iced Tea, 13 oz.	40.00	50.00
Tumbler, 4¾", 9 oz., Square Foot	60.00	65.00
Tumbler, 5¼", 10 oz., Footed	30.00	30.00
Tumbler, 6½", 12½ oz., Footed	95.00	110.00
Vase, 8"	45.00	40.00

QUEEN MARY, "VERTICAL RIBBED" ⊂═══════⊃
(pink, crystal)
HOCKING GLASS COMPANY, 1936 – 1940

	Pink	Crystal
Ashtray, 2" x 3¾", Oval	5.00	3.00
Bowl, 4", One Handle or None	5.00	4.00
Bowl, 5", Berry	14.00	7.00
Bowl, 6", Cereal	25.00	8.00
Bowl, 5½", Two Handles ...	20.00	5.00
Bowl, 8¾", Large Berry	20.00	10.00
Butter Dish or Preserve & Cover	150.00	26.00
Candy Dish & Cover	40.00	22.00
Candlesticks, 4½", Double Branch, Pr.	----	15.00
Celery or Pickle Dish, 5" x 10"	30.00	12.00
Cigarette Jar, Oval, 2" x 3"	10.00	6.00
Coaster, 3½"	6.00	2.50
Coaster/Ashtray, 4¼", Square	6.00	5.00
Compote, 5¾"	25.00	12.00

	Pink	Crystal
Creamer, Oval	12.00	6.50
Cup	8.00	5.00
Plate, 6" & 6⅝"	6.00	4.00
Plate, 8½", Salad	----	5.00
Plate, 9¾", Dinner..............	55.00	18.00
Plate, 12", Sandwich	22.00	10.00
Plate, 14", Serving Tray.....	22.00	12.00
Relish Tray, 12", 3-Part	20.00	10.00
Relish Tray, 14", 4-Part	20.00	12.00
Salt & Pepper, Pr.	----	22.00
Saucer................................	2.00	1.50
Sherbet, Footed.................	9.00	5.00
Sugar, Oval	10.00	6.50
Tumbler, 3½", Juice, 5 oz................................	14.00	4.00
Tumbler, 4", Water, 9 oz.................................	17.00	7.00
Tumbler, 5", 10 oz., Footed	70.00	33.00

RADIANCE
(red, cobalt and ice blue, amber, crystal)
NEW MARTINSVILLE, 1936 – 1939

	Red Blue	Amber
Bonbon, 6"	30.00	15.00
Bonbon, 6", Footed	32.00	17.50
Bonbon, 6", Covered	100.00	45.00
Bowl, 5", Two-Handled Nut	20.00	10.00
Bowl, 7", Two-Part	30.00	18.00
Bowl, 7', Pickle	25.00	15.00
Bowl, 8", Three-Part Relish	45.00	25.00
Bowl, 10", Celery	30.00	18.00
Bowl, 10", Crimped	45.00	25.00
Bowl, 10", Flared	45.00	22.00
Bowl, 12", Crimped	55.00	30.00
Bowl, 12", Flared	50.00	27.50
Butter Dish	475.00	210.00
Candlestick, 8", Pr.	225.00	75.00
Candle, Two-Light, Pr.	150.00	85.00
Cheese & Cracker, 11" Plate Set	110.00	30.00
Comport, 5"	32.00	18.00
Comport, 6"	38.00	22.00
Condiment Set, Four-Piece on Tray	325.00	150.00

	Red Blue	Amber
Creamer	25.00	15.00
Cruet, Individual	75.00	36.00
Cup	18.00	12.00
Decanter, Handled, w/Stopper	195.00	100.00
Lamp, 12"	110.00	60.00
Mayonnaise, Three-Piece Set	95.00	35.00
Pitcher, 64 oz.	295.00	150.00
Plate, 8", Luncheon	16.00	10.00
Plate, 14", Punch Bowl Liner	85.00	45.00
Punch Bowl	200.00	100.00
Punch Cup, Flat	15.00	7.00
Punch Ladle	135.00	95.00
Salt & Pepper, Pr.	95.00	50.00
Saucer	8.50	6.00
Sugar	25.00	15.00
Tray, Oval	40.00	24.00
Tumbler, 9 oz.	30.00	20.00
Vase, 10", Flared	100.00	45.00
Vase, 12", Crimped	150.00	55.00

RAINDROPS, "OPTIC DESIGN"
(green, crystal)
FEDERAL GLASS COMPANY, 1929 – 1933

	Green		Green
Bowl, 4½", Fruit	6.00	Sherbet	8.00
Bowl, 6", Cereal	10.00	Sugar	7.50
Bowl, 7½", Berry	50.00	Sugar Cover	40.00
Cup	6.00	Tumbler, 3", 4 oz.	5.00
Creamer	8.00	Tumbler, 3⅞", 5 oz.	7.00
Plate, 6", Sherbet	2.50	Tumbler, 4⅛", 9½ oz.	9.00
Plate, 8", Luncheon	6.00	Tumbler, 5", 10 oz.	9.00
Salt & Pepper, Pr.	325.00	Tumbler, 5⅜", 14 oz.	12.00
Saucer	2.00	Whiskey, 1⅞"	7.00

RIBBON
(green, black, crystal)
HAZEL ATLAS GLASS COMPANY, 1930 – 1932

	Green	Black		Green	Black
Bowl, 4", Berry	30.00	----	Plate, 8", Luncheon	5.00	14.00
Bowl, 5", Cereal	40.00	----	Salt & Pepper, Pr.	30.00	45.00
Bowl, 8", Large Berry	38.00	35.00	Saucer	2.50	----
Candy Dish & Cover	42.00	----	Sherbet, Footed	6.00	----
Creamer, Footed	15.00	----	Sugar, Footed	14.00	----
Cup	5.00	----	Tumbler, 6", 10 oz.	33.00	----
Plate, 6¼", Sherbet	3.00	----			

RING, "BANDED RINGS"
(crystal, green and crystal with decoration)
HOCKING GLASS COMPANY, 1927 – 1932

	Crystal	Green & Crystal w/dec.
Bowl, 5", Berry	4.00	7.00
Bowl, 7", Soup	11.00	15.00
Bowl, 8", Large Berry	10.00	15.00
Butter Tub or Ice Tub	22.00	40.00
Cocktail Shaker	20.00	30.00
Cup	4.50	6.00
Creamer, Footed	4.50	6.00
Decanter & Stopper	27.00	42.00
Goblet, 7" to 8" (varies), 9 oz.	7.50	15.00
Ice Bucket	22.00	35.00
Pitcher, 8", 60 oz.	17.50	25.00
Pitcher, 8½", 80 oz.	20.00	35.00
Plate, 6¼", Sherbet	2.00	2.50
Plate, 6½", Off-Center Ring	5.00	6.00
Plate, 8", Luncheon	2.50	4.50
* Salt & Pepper, 3", Pr.	22.00	45.00

	Crystal	Green & Crystal w/dec.
Sandwich Server, Center Handle	17.50	27.50
Saucer	1.50	2.00
Sherbet, Low (for 6½" Plate)	8.00	18.00
Sherbet, 4¾", Footed	5.00	9.00
Sugar, Footed	4.50	5.50
Tumbler, 3½", 5 oz.	5.00	6.50
Tumbler, 4¼", 9 oz.	4.50	10.00
Tumbler, 5⅛", 12 oz.	7.00	12.00
Tumbler, 3½", Footed Cocktail	6.00	10.00
Tumbler, 5½", Water, Footed	6.00	10.00
Tumbler, 6½", Iced Tea, Footed	8.00	15.00
Vase, 8"	17.50	38.00
Whiskey, 2", 1½ oz.	6.00	11.00

* Green – $55.00

ROCK CRYSTAL, "EARLY AMERICAN ROCK CRYSTAL"

(pink, green, cobalt, red, yellow, amber, blue-green, crystal)
McKEE GLASS COMPANY, 1920s and 1930s in color

	Crystal	Red
Bonbon, 7½", S.E.	22.00	60.00
Bowl, 4", 5", Fruit, S.E.	16.00	32.00
Bowl, 5", Finger Bowl w/7" Plate, P.E.	30.00	85.00
Bowl, 7", Pickle or Spoon Tray	25.00	65.00
Bowl, 7", 8", Salad, S.E.	26.00	75.00
Bowl, 9", 10½", Salad, S.E.	33.00	110.00
Bowl, 11½", Two-Part, Relish	30.00	75.00
Bowl, 12", Oblong Celery	30.00	90.00
Bowl, 12½", Footed Center Bowl	85.00	325.00
Bowl, 13", Roll Tray	40.00	125.00
Bowl, 14", Six-Part Relish	40.00	----
Candelabra, Two-Light, Pr.	45.00	295.00

	Crystal	Red
Candelabra, Three-Light, Pr.	55.00	350.00
Candlesticks, 5½", Low, Pr.	40.00	175.00
Candlesticks, 8½", Tall, Pr.	100.00	425.00
Candy & Cover, Round	60.00	250.00
Cake Stand, 11", Footed, 2¾" High	37.00	125.00
Compote, 7"	38.00	95.00
Creamer, 9 oz., Footed	20.00	70.00
Cruet & Stopper, Oil, 6 oz.	97.50	----
Cup, 7 oz.	17.50	70.00
Goblet, 7½", 8 oz., Low Footed	18.00	57.50
Goblet, 11 oz., Iced Tea, Low Footed	20.00	67.50
Jelly, 5", Footed, S.E.	18.00	52.50

S.E. – McKee designation for scalloped edge
P.E. – McKee designation for plain edge

ROCK CRYSTAL, "EARLY AMERICAN ROCK CRYSTAL"

	Crystal	Red
Lamp, Electric	225.00	695.00
Parfait, 3½ oz., Low Foot	25.00	75.00
Pitcher, ½ Gal., 7½" High	125.00	----
Pitcher, Large, Covered	195.00	750.00
Plate, 6", Bread & Butter, S.E.	6.00	20.00
Plate, 7½", 8½", Salad, P.E. & S.E.	9.00	22.00
Plate, 9", 10½", 11½", Cake, S.E. (small center design)	20.00	60.00
Plate, 10½", Dinner, S.E. (large center design)	50.00	175.00
Salt & Pepper, Two Styles	75.00	----
Salt Dip	40.00	----
Sandwich Server, Center Handled	30.00	145.00
Saucer	7.50	22.00
Sherbet or Egg, 3½ oz., Footed	18.00	65.00
Stemware, 1 oz., Footed Cordial	22.00	65.00
Stemware, 2 oz., 3 oz., Footed Wines	20.00	55.00
Stemware, 3½ oz., Footed Cocktail	15.00	40.00
Stemware, 6 oz., Footed Champagne	16.00	35.00
Stemware, 8 oz., Large Footed Goblet	18.00	60.00
Sundae, 6 oz., Low Footed	12.00	35.00
Sugar, 10 oz., Open, Flat	15.00	----
Sugar, 10 oz., Covered, Footed	45.00	175.00
Tumbler, Whiskey, 2½ oz.	20.00	65.00
Tumbler, Juice, 5 oz.	20.00	57.50
Tumbler, Old Fashioned, 5 oz.	20.00	60.00
Tumbler, 9 oz., Concave or Straight	18.00	52.50
Tumbler, 12 oz., Concave or Straight	25.00	67.50
Vase, 11", Footed	60.00	195.00

S.E. – McKee designation for scalloped edge
P.E. – McKee designation for plain edge

ROSE CAMEO
(green)
BELMONT TUMBLER COMPANY, 1931

	Green		Green
Bowl, 4½", Berry	15.00	Plate, 7", Salad	14.00
Bowl, 5", Cereal	20.00	Sherbet	14.00
Bowl, 6", Straight Side	25.00	Tumbler, 5", Footed, Two Styles	25.00

ROSEMARY, "DUTCH ROSE"
(pink, green, amber)
FEDERAL GLASS COMPANY 1935 – 1937

	Amber	Green		Amber	Green
Bowl, 5", Berry	6.00	9.00	Plate, 6¾", Salad	6.00	9.50
Bowl, 5", Cream Soup	18.00	25.00	Plate, Dinner	10.00	15.00
Bowl, 6", Cereal	30.00	35.00	Plate, Grill	10.00	15.00
Bowl, 10",			Platter, 12", Oval	18.00	22.00
Oval Vegetable	18.00	30.00	Saucer	4.00	6.00
Creamer, Footed	9.00	12.50	Sugar, Footed	9.00	12.50
Cup	7.50	9.50	Tumbler, 4¼", 9 oz.	32.00	35.00

ROULETTE, "MANY WINDOWS"
(pink, green)
HOCKING GLASS COMPANY, 1935 – 1939

	Pink	Green		Pink	Green
Bowl, 9", Fruit	25.00	25.00	Tumbler, 3¼", Old Fashioned, 7½ oz.	35.00	45.00
Cup	----	7.00	Tumbler, 4⅛", Water, 9 oz.	30.00	30.00
Pitcher, 8", 64 oz.	40.00	45.00			
Plate, 6", Sherbet	----	5.00	Tumbler, 5⅛", Iced Tea, 12 oz.	28.00	30.00
Plate, 8½", Luncheon	----	7.00			
Plate, 12", Sandwich	----	16.00	Tumbler, 5½", 10 oz., Footed	----	35.00
Saucer	----	3.50			
Sherbet	----	8.00	Whiskey, 2½", 1½ oz.	17.00	17.00
Tumbler, 3¼", Juice, 5 oz.	25.00	25.00			

"ROUND ROBIN"
(green, iridescent)
1927 – 1932

	Green	Iridescent		Green	Iridescent
Bowl, 4", Berry	10.00	9.00	Plate, 8", Luncheon	4.00	4.00
Cup, Footed	7.00	7.00	Plate, 12", Sandwich	12.00	10.00
Creamer, Footed	10.00	9.00	Saucer	2.00	2.00
Domino Tray	100.00	----	Sherbet	9.00	10.00
Plate, 6", Sherbet	2.50	2.50	Sugar	10.00	9.00

ROXANA
(yellow, white, crystal)
HAZEL ATLAS GLASS COMPANY, 1932

	Yellow		Yellow
Bowl, 4½" x 2⅜"	15.00	Plate, 6" 10.00	
Bowl, 5", Berry	15.00	Sherbet, Footed 12.00	
Bowl, 6", Cereal	20.00	Tumbler, 4", 9 oz. 22.00	
Plate, 5½"	10.00		

ROYAL LACE

(See Reproduction Section, Page 183) (pink, green, crystal, blue)
HAZEL ATLAS GLASS COMPANY, 1934 – 1941

	Pink	Blue
Bowl, 4¾", Cream Soup ..	30.00	48.00
Bowl, 5", Berry	33.00	55.00
Bowl, 10", Round Berry ...	35.00	65.00
Bowl, 10", Three-Leg, Straight Edge	55.00	95.00
Bowl, 10", Three-Leg, Rolled Edge..................	95.00	600.00
Bowl, 10", Three-Leg, Ruffled Edge	95.00	700.00
Bowl, 11", Oval Vegetable	35.00	65.00
Butter Dish & Cover	195.00	650.00
Candlesticks, Straight Edge, Pr.	65.00	165.00
Candlesticks, Rolled Edge, Pr.	135.00	500.00
Candlesticks, Ruffled Edge, Pr.	135.00	500.00
* Cookie Jar & Cover	60.00	375.00
Creamer, Footed	22.00	60.00
Cup...................................	20.00	40.00

	Pink	Blue
Nut Dish............................	425.00	1,575.00
Pitcher, 48 oz., Straight Sides	90.00	195.00
Pitcher, 8", 68 oz..............	115.00	275.00
Pitcher, 8", 86 oz..............	135.00	325.00
Pitcher, 8½", 96 oz...........	150.00	425.00
Plate, 6", Sherbet	9.00	15.00
Plate, 8½", Luncheon.......	16.00	38.00
Plate, 9⅞", Dinner	30.00	45.00
Plate, 9⅞", Grill	22.00	40.00
Platter, 13", Oval	40.00	60.00
Salt & Pepper, Pr..............	65.00	295.00
Saucer	7.00	12.50
Sherbet, Footed	20.00	50.00
Sugar	15.00	40.00
Sugar Lid	60.00	195.00
Tumbler, 3½", 5 oz...........	33.00	60.00
Tumbler, 4⅛", 9 oz...........	28.00	50.00
Tumbler, 4⅞", 10 oz.........	75.00	130.00
Tumbler, 5⅜", 12 oz.........	65.00	120.00

* Beware of Reproductions

ROYAL RUBY
(red)
ANCHOR HOCKING GLASS COMPANY, 1939 – 1960s

	Red
Ashtray, 4½", Square	5.00
Bowl, 4¼", Berry	5.50
Bowl, 5¼"	13.00
Bowl, 7½", Soup	12.50
Bowl, 8", Oval Vegetable	30.00
Bowl, 8½", Large Berry	17.50
Bowl, 10", Deep	40.00
Bowl, 11½", Salad	33.00
Card Holder	65.00
Creamer, Flat	12.00
Creamer, Footed	9.00
Cup (Round or Square)	6.00
Goblet, Ball Stem	12.00
Lamp	35.00
Pitcher, 42 oz., Tilted or Upright	35.00
Pitcher, 3 Qt., Tilted	35.00
Pitcher, 3 Qt., Upright	40.00
Plate, 6½", Sherbet	4.00
Plate, 7", Salad	5.00

	Red
Plate, 7¾", Luncheon	6.00
Plate, 9" or 9¼", Dinner	11.00
Plate, 13¾"	25.00
Punch Bowl & Stand	77.50
Punch Cup	3.00
Saucer (Round or Square)	2.50
Sherbet, Footed	8.00
Sugar, Flat	12.00
Sugar, Footed	8.00
Sugar Lid	10.00
Tumbler, 2½", Footed Wine	14.00
Tumbler, 3½", Cocktail	12.50
Tumbler, 5 oz., Juice, Two Styles	7.50
Tumbler, 9 oz., Water	6.50
Tumbler, 13 oz., Iced Tea	15.00
Vase, 4", Ball-Shaped	6.00
Vase, 6½", Bulbous, Tall	9.00
Vases, Several Styles (small)	6.00
Vases, 9", Two Styles	17.50

"S" PATTERN, "STIPPLED ROSE BAND"
(crystal, amber)
MacBETH-EVANS GLASS COMPANY, 1930 – 1933

	Crystal	Amber		Crystal	Amber
Bowl, 5½", Cereal	5.00	9.00	Plate, 11", Heavy Cake	40.00	50.00
Bowl, 8½", Large Berry	13.00	18.00	Plate, 13", Heavy Cake	65.00	75.00
Creamer, Thick or Thin	6.00	7.00	Saucer	2.00	2.50
Cup, Thick or Thin	3.50	5.00	Sherbet, Low Footed	4.50	7.50
Pitcher, 80 oz.	55.00	125.00	Sugar, Thick & Thin	5.50	6.50
Plate, 6", Sherbet	2.50	3.00	Tumbler, 3½", 5 oz.	5.00	7.00
Plate, 8", Luncheon	5.00	6.00	Tumbler, 4", 9 oz.	6.00	8.00
Plate, 9¼", Dinner	----	10.00	Tumbler, 4¼", 10 oz.	8.00	9.00
Plate, Grill	6.50	8.00	Tumbler, 5", 12 oz.	10.00	15.00

SANDWICH

(See Reproduction Section, Page 184)
(crystal, 1930 – 1960s; amber [desert gold], 1960s; pink and ruby red, 1939 – 1940; forest green, 1950 – 1960s; white [opaque], 1950s)
HOCKING GLASS COMPANY, 1939 – 1964

	Crystal	Green		Crystal	Green
Bowl, 4⅞", Berry	6.00	6.00	Plate, 7", Dessert	12.00	----
Bowl, 6½", Smooth or			Plate, 8"	7.00	----
Scalloped	7.50	60.00	Plate, 9", Dinner	20.00	140.00
Bowl, 6¾", Cereal	50.00	----	Plate, 9" Indent for		
Bowl, 7", Salad	7.00	75.00	Punch Cup	5.00	----
Bowl, 8", Smooth or			Plate, 12", Sandwich	40.00	----
Scalloped	12.00	100.00	Punch Bowl, 9¾"	20.00	----
Bowl, 8¼", Oval	8.00	----	Punch Stand	33.00	----
Butter Dish, Low	45.00	----	Punch Cup	2.25	----
Cookie Jar & Cover	40.00	----	Saucer	1.50	20.00
Creamer	6.00	30.00	Sherbet, Footed	8.00	----
Cup, Tea or Coffee	2.50	20.00	Sugar & Cover	24.00	27.50 *
Custard Cup	3.50	3.00	Tumbler, 5 oz., Juice	6.50	4.00
Custard Cup Liner	21.00	2.50	Tumbler, 9 oz., Water	8.00	5.00
Pitcher, 6", Juice	65.00	225.00	Tumbler, 9 oz., Footed	35.00	----
Pitcher, ½ gal., Ice Lip	85.00	495.00	* No Lid		

SANDWICH

(See Reproduction Section, Page 185)
(crystal, amber, pink, red, teal blue, light green)
INDIANA GLASS COMPANY, 1920 – 1970s

	Crystal	Pink
Ashtray Set (Club, Spade, Heart, Diamond Shapes) each	3.50	----
Bowl, 4¼", Berry	3.50	----
Bowl, 6"	4.00	----
Bowl, 6", Six Sides	5.00	----
Bowl, 8½"	12.00	----
Bowl, 9", Console	16.00	40.00
Bowl, 11½", Console	20.00	50.00
Butter Dish & Cover, Domed	22.50	----
Candlesticks, 3½", Pr.	17.50	45.00
Candlesticks, 7", Pr.	30.00	----
Creamer	9.00	----
Cruet, 6½" & Stopper	27.50	----
Cup	4.00	----
Creamer & Sugar on Diamond-Shaped Tray	16.00	----
Decanter & Stopper	22.50	125.00
Goblet, 9 oz.	13.00	----

	Crystal	Pink
Pitcher, 68 oz.	22.50	----
Plate, 6", Sherbet	3.00	----
Plate, 7", Bread & Butter	4.00	----
Plate, 8", Oval, Indent for Sherbet	5.50	----
Plate, 8⅜", Luncheon	5.00	----
Plate, 10½", Dinner	8.00	18.00
Plate, 13", Sandwich	13.00	25.00
Sandwich Server, Center Handle	18.00	27.50
Saucer	2.00	----
Sherbet	6.00	15.00
Sugar	9.00	----
Tumbler, 3 oz., Footed Cocktail	7.50	----
Tumbler, 8 oz., Footed Water	9.00	----
Tumbler, 12 oz., Footed Iced Tea	10.00	----
Wine, 3", 4 oz.	6.00	22.50

SHARON, "CABBAGE ROSE"
(See Reproduction Section, Page 186 – 188)
(pink, green, amber, crystal)
FEDERAL GLASS COMPANY, 1935 – 1939

	Amber	Pink
Bowl, 5", Berry	8.50	15.00
Bowl, 5", Cream Soup	28.00	50.00
Bowl, 6", Cereal	22.00	28.00
Bowl, 7½", Flat Soup, 2" Deep	52.50	60.00
Bowl, 8½", Large Berry	6.00	35.00
Bowl, 9½", Oval Vegetable	20.00	35.00
Bowl, 10½", Fruit	22.50	45.00
Butter Dish & Cover	47.50	60.00
Cake Plate, Footed, 11½"	25.00	45.00
Candy Jar & Cover	45.00	50.00
Cheese Dish & Cover	210.00	1,250.00
Creamer, Footed	14.00	20.00
Cup	9.00	14.00
Jam Dish, 7½"	40.00	260.00
Pitcher, 80 oz., with or without Ice Lip	140.00	185.00

	Amber	Pink
Plate, 6", Bread & Butter	5.00	7.50
Plate, 7½", Salad	15.00	23.00
Plate, 9½", Dinner	12.00	20.00
Platter, 12½", Oval	20.00	32.00
Salt & Pepper, Pr.	40.00	55.00
Saucer	6.50	12.00
Sherbet, Footed	13.00	18.00
Sugar	9.00	14.00
Sugar Lid	22.00	33.00
Tumbler, 4⅛", 9 oz., Thin	30.00	42.00
Tumbler, 4⅛", 9 oz., Thick	30.00	42.00
Tumbler, 5¼", 12 oz., Thin	55.00	52.00
Tumbler, 5¼", 12 oz., Thick	65.00	85.00
Tumbler, 6½", Footed, 15 oz.	110.00	57.50

SHELL PINK MILK GLASS
JEANNETTE GLASS CO., 1957 – 1959

	Opaque Pink		Opaque Pink
Ashtray, Butterfly Shape	30.00	"Napco" #2250, Ftd. Bowl w/Berries	15.00
Base, for Lazy Susan, w/Ball Bearings	160.00	"Napco" #2255, Ftd. Bowl w/Saw Tooth Top	25.00
Bowl, 6½", Wedding, w/Cover	22.50	"Napco" #2256, Square Comport	12.50
Bowl, 8", Pheasant, Ftd.	37.50	"National" Candy Bottom	12.50
Bowl, 8", Wedding, w/Cover	27.50	Pitcher, 24 oz., Ftd., Thumbprint	27.50
Bowl, 9", Ftd., Fruit Stand, Floragold	27.50	Powder Jar, 4¾", w/Cover	45.00
Bowl, 10", Florentine, Ftd.	30.00	Punch Base, 3½", Tall	45.00
Bowl, 10½", ftd., Holiday	45.00	Punch Bowl, 7½ qt	85.00
Bowl, 10⅞", 4 ftd., Lombardi, Designed Center	42.00	Punch Cup, 5 oz. (also fits snack tray)	6.00
Bowl, 10⅞", 4 Ftd., Lombardi, Plain Center	27.00	Punch Ladle, Pink Plastic	25.00
Bowl, 17½", Gondola Fruit	40.00	Punch Set, 15 Pc. (Bowl, Base, 12 Cups, Ladle)	225.00
Cake Plate, Anniversary	250.00	Relish, 12", 4 Part, Octagonal, Vineyard Design	42.00
Cake Stand, 10", Harp	45.00	Stem, 5 oz., Sherbet, Thumbprint	10.00
Candle Holder, 2 Light, Pr.	45.00	Stem, 8 oz., Water Goblet, Thumbprint	12.50
Candle Holder, Eagle, 3 Ftd., Pr.	85.00	Sugar Cover	17.50
Candy Dish w/Cover, 6½" High, Square	30.00	Sugar, Ftd., Baltimore Pear Design	12.00
Candy Dish, 4 Ftd., 5¼", Floragold	20.00	Tray, 7¾" x 10", Snack w/Cup Indent	9.00
Candy Jar, 5½", 4 Ftd., w/Cover, Grapes	20.00	Tray, 12½" x 9¾", 2 Hndl., Harp	60.00
Celery and Relish, 12½", 3 Part	45.00	Tray, 13½", Lazy Susan, 5 Part	75.00
Cigarette Box, Butterfly Finial	235.00	Tray, 15¾", 5 Part, 2 Hndl.	85.00
Compote, 6", Windsor	20.00	Tray, 16½", 6 Part, Venetian	40.00
Cookie Jar w/Cover, 6½" High	110.00	Tray,Lazy Susan Complete w/Base	245.00
Creamer, Baltimore Pear Design	15.00	Tumbler, 5 oz., Juice, Ftd., Thumbprint	8.00
Honey Jar, Beehive Shape, Notched Cover	40.00	Vase, 5", Cornucopia	15.00
"Napco" #2249, Cross Hatch Design Pot	15.00	Vase, 7"	35.00
		Vase, 9", Heavy Bottom	135.00

SIERRA, "PINWHEEL"
(pink, green)
JEANNETTE GLASS COMPANY, 1931 – 1933

	Pink	Green
Bowl, 5½", Cereal	16.00	18.00
Bowl, 8½", Large Berry	35.00	32.00
Bowl, 9½", Oval Vegetable	65.00	125.00
Butter Dish & Cover	70.00	70.00
Creamer	20.00	23.00
Cup	13.00	16.00
Pitcher, 6½", 32 oz.	115.00	140.00
Plate, 9", Dinner	22.00	25.00
Platter, 11", Oval	55.00	65.00
Salt & Pepper, Pr.	45.00	45.00
Saucer	8.00	9.00
Serving Tray, Two Handles	20.00	20.00
Sugar	22.00	28.00
Sugar Cover	18.00	19.00
Tumbler, 4½", 9 oz., Footed	65.00	85.00

SPIRAL
(green, crystal)
HOCKING GLASS COMPANY, 1928 – 1930

	Green
Bowl, 4¾", Berry	5.00
Bowl, 7", Mixing	12.00
Bowl, 8", Large Berry	12.50
Creamer, Flat or Footed	8.00
Cup	5.00
Ice or Butter Tub	30.00
Pitcher, 7⅝", 58 oz.	35.00
Plate, 6", Sherbet	2.50
Plate, 8", Luncheon	4.00
Platter	33.00
Preserve & Cover	35.00

	Green
Salt & Pepper, Pr.	35.00
Sandwich Server, Center Handle	25.00
Saucer	2.50
Sherbet	4.00
Sugar, Flat or Footed	8.00
Tumbler, 3", Juice, 5 oz.	4.50
Tumbler, 5", Water, 9 oz.	7.50
Tumber, 5⅞", Footed	18.00
Vase, 5¾", Footed	50.00

STAR
(amber, crystal and crystal w/gold trim)
FEDERAL GLASS COMPANY, 1950s

	Amber/Crystal		Amber/Crystal
Bowl, 4⅝", Dessert	4.00	Plate, 9⅜", Dinner	5.00
Bowl, 8⅜", Vegetable	10.00	Plate, 11¾", Sandwich	12.00
Butter Dish, Round	95.00	Saucer	4.00
Creamer	9.00	Sugar	6.00
Cup	10.00	Sugar Lid	6.00
Pitcher, 5¾", 36 oz., Juice	8.00	Tumbler, 2¼", 1½ oz., Whiskey	3.00
Pitcher, 7", 60 oz.	12.00	Tumbler, 3⅜", 4½ oz., Juice	4.00
Pitcher, 9¼", 85 oz., Ice Lip	15.00	Tumbler, 3⅞", 9 oz., Water	6.00
Plate, 6³⁄₁₆", Salad	3.00	Tumbler, 5⅛", 12 oz., Iced Tea	10.00

STARLIGHT
(pink, white, crystal, cobalt blue)
HAZEL ATLAS GLASS COMPANY, 1938 – 1940

	Crystal	Pink		Crystal	Pink
Bowl, 5½", Cereal	7.00	12.00	Plate, 9", Dinner	8.00	----
Bowl, 8½", Closed Handles	10.00	20.00	Plate, 13", Sandwich	15.00	20.00
Bowl, 11½", Salad	30.00	----	Relish Dish	15.00	----
Creamer, Oval	8.00	----	Salt & Pepper, Pr.	22.50	----
Cup	5.00	----	Saucer	2.00	----
Plate, 6", Bread & Butter	3.00	----	Sherbet	15.00	----
Plate, 8½", Luncheon	5.00	----	Sugar, Oval	8.00	----

STRAWBERRY
(pink, green, iridescent)
U.S. GLASS COMPANY, 1928 – 1931

	Pink or Green		Pink or Green
Bowl, 4", Berry	12.00	Pickle Dish	20.00
Bowl, 6¼", 2" Deep	125.00	Pitcher, 7¾"	195.00
Bowl, 6½", Deep Salad	25.00	Plate, 6", Sherbet	12.00
Bowl, 7½", Deep Berry	30.00	Plate, 7½", Salad	18.00
Butter Dish & Cover	195.00	Sherbet	10.00
Compote, 5¾"	25.00	Sugar, Small, Open	22.00
Creamer, Small	22.00	Sugar, Large	40.00
Creamer, Large, 4⅝"	40.00	Sugar Cover	65.00
Olive Dish, 5", One Handle	20.00	Tumbler, 3⅝", 9 oz.	38.00

SUNBURST

JEANNETTE GLASS COMPANY, Late 1920s

	Crystal
Bowl, 4¾", Berry	9.00
Bowl, 8½", Berry	20.00
Bowl, 11"	25.00
Candlesticks, Double, Pr.	30.00
Creamer, Footed	10.00
Cup	10.00
Plate, 5½"	7.00

	Crystal
Plate, 9¼", Dinner	22.00
Plate, 11¾", Sandwich	20.00
Relish, 2 Part	12.00
Saucer	4.00
Sherbet	15.00
Sugar	10.00
Tumbler, 4", 9 oz., Flat	25.00

SUNFLOWER
(pink, green, ultramarine)
JEANNETTE GLASS COMPANY, Late 1920s

	Pink	Green		Pink	Green
Ashtray, 5", Center Design Only	9.00	12.00	Saucer	10.00	12.00
Cake Plate, 10", Three			Sugar	22.00	25.00
Legs	15.00	15.00	Tumbler, 4¾", 8 oz., Footed	35.00	35.00
Creamer	22.00	25.00	Trivet, 7", Three Legs,		
Cup	16.00	18.00	Turned-Up Edge	325.00	350.00
Plate, 9", Dinner	22.00	25.00			

SWIRL, "PETAL SWIRL"
(pink, ultramarine, delphite)
JEANNETTE GLASS COMPANY, 1937 – 1938

	Pink	Ultramarine		Pink	Ultramarine
Bowl, 5¼", Cereal....	14.00	18.00	Plate, 7¼"	10.00	15.00
Bowl, 9", Salad........	20.00	30.00	Plate, 8", Salad........	10.00	15.00
Bowl, 10", Footed,			Plate, 9¼", Dinner....	17.00	22.00
Closed Handles...	35.00	35.00	Plate, 12½",		
Bowl, 10½",			Sandwich.............	22.00	32.00
Console, Footed	22.00	30.00	Salt & Pepper, Pr.....	----	45.00
Butter Dish...............	210.00	285.00	Saucer.....................	3.00	5.00
Candleholders,			Sherbet, Low		
Double Branch, Pr..	70.00	60.00	Footed	17.00	25.00
Candy Dish, Open,			Soup, Tab Handles		
Three Legs	15.00	20.00	(Lug).....................	35.00	40.00
Candy Dish w/Cover.	120.00	180.00	Sugar, Footed..........	10.00	16.00
Coaster, 1" x 3¼"	13.00	16.00	Tumbler, 4", 9 oz.	22.00	35.00
Creamer, Footed......	10.00	16.00	Tumbler, 5⅛", 13 oz..	55.00	120.00
Cup	10.00	16.00	Tumbler, 9 oz.,		
Pitcher, 48 oz.,			Footed	22.00	45.00
Footed	----	1,850.00	Vase, 6½", Footed ...	23.00	----
Plate, 6½", Sherbet .	7.00	8.00	Vase, 8½", Footed ...	----	30.00

TEA ROOM
(green, pink, crystal, amber)
INDIANA GLASS COMPANY, 1926 – 1931

	Green	Pink		Green	Pink
Bowl, Finger	60.00	60.00	Plate, 8¼", Luncheon	35.00	30.00
Bowl, 7½", Banana Split	120.00	115.00	Plate, 10½",		
Bowl, 8½", Celery	35.00	27.50	Two-Handled	50.00	45.00
Bowl, 8¾", Deep Salad	95.00	75.00	Relish, Divided	25.00	20.00
Bowl, 9½",			Salt & Pepper, Pr.	65.00	50.00
Oval Vegetable	75.00	65.00	Saucer	30.00	30.00
Candlestick, Low, Pr.	80.00	95.00	Sherbet, Three Styles	25.00	22.00
Creamer, 4"	26.00	26.00	Sugar, 4"	20.00	18.00
Creamer & Sugar			Sugar, Flat w/Cover	195.00	160.00
on Tray, 3½"	85.00	75.00	Sundae, Footed, Ruffled	95.00	75.00
Cup	60.00	60.00	Tumbler, 8½ oz., Flat	110.00	120.00
Goblet, 9 oz.	75.00	65.00	Tumbler, 6 oz., Footed	35.00	35.00
Ice Bucket	60.00	55.00	Tumbler, 8 oz., Footed	33.00	33.00
Lamp, Electric	135.00	110.00	Tumbler, 11 oz., Footed	50.00	45.00
Mustard, Covered	195.00	160.00	Tumbler, 12 oz., Footed	75.00	65.00
Parfait	95.00	95.00	Vase, 9"	75.00	70.00
Pitcher, 64 oz.	175.00	150.00	Vase, 11", Ruffled Edge	250.00	300.00
Plate, 6½", Sherbet	32.50	30.00	Vase, 11", Straight	150.00	150.00

THISTLE
(pink, green, crystal)
MacBETH-EVANS, 1929 – 1930

	Pink	Green
Bowl, 5½", Cereal	28.00	30.00
Bowl, 10¼", Large Fruit	395.00	250.00
Cup, Thin	25.00	28.00
Plate, 8", Luncheon	20.00	22.00

	Pink	Green
Plate, 10¼", Grill	25.00	30.00
Plate, 13", Cake, Heavy	150.00	195.00
Saucer	12.00	12.00

TULIP

(amethyst, blue, green, crystal)
DELL GLASS COMPANY, Early 1930s

	Amethyst, Blue,	Green, Crystal
Bowl, Oval, Oblong, 13¼".	110.00	90.00
Candleholder, 3¾", Pr. (like sherbet)	70.00	50.00
Candy w/Lid	150.00	100.00
Creamer	22.00	20.00
Cup	22.00	14.00
Decanter w/Stopper	195.00	150.00
Ice Tub, 4⅞" Wide, 3" Deep.	95.00	65.00

	Amethyst, Blue,	Green, Crystal
Plate, 6"	10.00	9.00
Plate, 7¼"	15.00	10.00
Plate, 10"	38.00	33.00
Saucer	8.00	6.00
Sherbet, 3¾", Flat	22.00	20.00
Sugar	22.00	20.00
Tumbler, Juice	28.00	22.00
Tumbler, Whiskey	30.00	25.00

TWISTED OPTIC
(pink, green, amber, crystal, yellow)
IMPERIAL GLASS COMPANY, 1927 – 1930

	Pink or Green
Bowl, 4¾", Cream Soup	12.00
Bowl, 5", Cereal	7.00
Bowl, 7", Salad or Soup	12.00
Candlestick, 3", Pr.	25.00
Candy Jar & Cover	35.00
Creamer	9.00
Cup	5.00
Pitcher, 64 oz.	35.00
Plate, 6", Sherbet	2.00
Plate, 7", Salad	3.50
Plate, 7½" x 9", Oval	6.00
Plate, 8", Luncheon	3.50
Preserve (Same as Candy but w/slot in lid)	30.00
Sandwich Server, Center Handle	22.00
Sandwich Server, Two-Handled, Flat	15.00
Saucer	2.00
Sherbet	7.00
Sugar	6.50
Tumbler, 4½", 9 oz.	8.00
Tumbler, 5¼", 12 oz.	10.00

U.S. SWIRL
(pink, green)
U.S. GLASS COMPANY, Late 1920s

	Green	Pink
Bowl, 4⅜", Berry	6.00	7.00
Bowl, 5½", One-Handled	10.00	11.00
Bowl, 7⅛", Large Berry	15.00	16.00
Bowl, 8¼", Oval	45.00	45.00
Butter & Cover	120.00	120.00
Butter Bottom	90.00	90.00
Butter Top	30.00	30.00
Candy w/Cover, Two-Handled	27.50	35.00

	Green	Pink
Creamer	14.00	16.00
Pitcher, 8", 48 oz.	65.00	65.00
Plate, 6⅛", Sherbet	2.50	2.50
Plate, 7⅞", Salad	6.00	7.00
Salt & Pepper, Pr.	60.00	60.00
Sherbet, 3¼"	5.00	6.00
Sugar w/Lid	35.00	40.00
Tumbler, 4⅝", 12 oz.	14.00	15.00
Vase, 6½"	30.00	25.00

"VICTORY"

(amber, green, pink, cobalt blue)
DIAMOND GLASS-WARE COMPANY, 1929 – 1932

	Pink	Blue
Bonbon, 7"	12.00	20.00
Bowl, 6½", Cereal	12.00	32.00
Bowl, 8½", Flat soup	20.00	50.00
Bowl, 9", Oval Vegetable	32.00	100.00
Bowl, 11", Rolled Edge	28.00	50.00
Bowl, 12", Console	35.00	65.00
Bowl, 12½", Flat Edge	30.00	65.00
Candlestick, 3", Pr.	30.00	110.00
Cheese & Cracker Set, 12" Indented Plate & Compote	40.00	----
Comport, 6" Tall, 6¾" Diameter	17.50	----
Creamer	15.00	50.00
Cup	10.00	35.00

	Pink	Blue
Goblet, 5", 7 oz.	20.00	----
Gravy Boat & Platter	200.00	350.00
Mayonnaise Set: 3½" Tall, 5½" Across, 8½" Indented Plate w/Ladle	42.50	110.00
Plate, 6", Bread & Butter	6.00	17.50
Plate, 7", Salad	7.00	20.00
Plate, 8", Luncheon	7.00	30.00
Plate, 9", Dinner	20.00	45.00
Platter, 12"	30.00	85.00
Sandwich Server, Center Handle	30.00	85.00
Saucer	4.00	12.50
Sherbet, Footed	14.00	28.00
Sugar	15.00	50.00

VITROCK ("FLOWER RIM")
(white)
ANCHOR HOCKING GLASS COMPANY, 1934 – Late 1930s

	White		White
Bowl, 4", Berry	5.00	Plate, 7¼", Salad	2.50
Bowl, 5½", Cream Soup	16.00	Plate, 8¾", Luncheon	4.50
Bowl, 6", Fruit	5.50	Plate, 9", Soup	32.00
Bowl, 7½", Cereal	6.00	Plate, 10", Dinner	9.00
Bowl, Vegetable	15.00	Platter, 11½"	33.00
Creamer, Oval	6.00	Saucer	2.50
Cup	4.00	Sugar, Oval	6.00

WATERFORD, "WAFFLE"
(crystal, pink)
HOCKING GLASS COMPANY, 1938 – 1944

	Crystal	Pink
Ashtray	7.50	----
Bowl, 4¾", Berry	6.50	18.00
Bowl, 5½", Cereal	19.00	40.00
Bowl, 8¼", Large Berry	10.00	25.00
Butter Dish & Cover	25.00	225.00
Coaster, 4"	3.50	----
Creamer, Oval	5.00	15.00
Cup	6.00	15.00
Goblet, 5¼", 5⅝"	16.00	----
Pitcher, Juice, 42 oz., Tilted	24.00	----
Pitcher, 80 oz., Ice Lip, Tilted	32.50	150.00

	Crystal	Pink
Plate, 6", Sherbet	3.00	7.00
Plate, 7⅛", Salad	6.00	12.50
Plate, 9⅝", Dinner	11.00	28.00
Plate, 10¼", Handled Cake	10.00	18.00
Plate, 13¾", Sandwich	13.00	33.00
Salt & Pepper, Two Types.	8.50	----
Saucer	2.00	6.00
Sherbet, Footed	4.00	18.00
Sugar	5.00	12.50
Sugar Cover, Oval	5.00	30.00
Tumbler, 4⅞", 10 oz., Footed	14.00	25.00

WINDSOR, "WINDSOR DIAMOND"
(pink, green, crystal)
JEANNETTE GLASS COMPANY, 1932 – 1946

	Crystal	Pink
Ashtray, 5¾"	13.50	42.00
Bowl, 4¾", Berry	4.00	10.00
Bowl, 5", Cream Soup	7.00	24.00
Bowl, 5⅛", 5⅜", Cereals	8.50	25.00
Bowl, 7⅛", Three Legs	8.00	30.00
Bowl, 8½", Large Berry	7.00	22.00
Bowl, 9½", Oval Vegetable	8.00	25.00
Bowl, 12½", Fruit Console	30.00	135.00
Bowl, 7" x 11¾", Boat Shape	20.00	38.00
Butter Dish	27.50	60.00
Cake Plate, 10¾", ftd.	9.00	25.00
Candlesticks, 3", Pr.	22.00	85.00
Candy Jar & Cover	20.00	----
Coaster, 3¼"	3.50	15.00
Compote	10.00	----
Creamer	5.00	14.00
Cup	3.50	10.00
Pitcher, 4½", 16 oz.	25.00	125.00

	Crystal	Pink
Pitcher, 6¾", 52 oz.	15.00	35.00
Plate, 6", Sherbet	2.50	8.00
Plate, 7", Salad	5.00	25.00
Plate, 9", Dinner	6.00	25.00
Plate, 10¼", Sandwich, Handled	6.00	16.00
Plate, 13⅝", Chop	12.00	35.00
Platter, 11½", Oval	8.00	22.00
Relish Platter, 11½", Divided	15.00	225.00
Salt & Pepper, Pr.	17.50	40.00
Saucer	2.00	5.00
Sherbet, Footed	4.00	12.00
Sugar & Cover	12.00	32.00
Tray, 4" Square	5.00	10.00
Tray, 4⅛" x 9"	5.00	10.00
Tray, 8½" x 9¾"	6.50	24.00
Tumbler, 3¼", 5 oz.	8.00	25.00
Tumbler, 4", 9 oz.	7.00	20.00
Tumbler, 5", 12 oz.	10.00	33.00
Tumbler, 7¼", Footed	18.00	---

REPRODUCTIONS

As popularity of any item in the collecting field grows, there is always someone or some company that will take advantage of the collector. This section will show you the reproductions in Depression Glass through March 2000.

Know your glassware and your dealer before spending your hard-earned cash for it; also, be wary of deals that seem too good to be true.

The items pictured in this section have all been reproduced since 1973 either by the original glass companies themselves or by private individuals.

Items introduced by companies are usually available in the local dish barns or merchant stores. Those privately manufactured are found at flea markets, local antique or junk shops, and auctions.

Some of the glass is marketed through private sales or parties much like the "Tupperware" parties. In these, the buyer is treated to "exclusive lines" of glassware.

My personal feeling is that as long as people buy these reproductions, re-issues, new products made to look old, or what have you, then they will continue to be made either privately or by the companies themselves. I feel also that buying a collectible is an investment; but buying a reproduction is merely speculation. These latter products appeal to me as much as swamp land in Florida.

What can we do? First, we can educate ourselves to know glass; secondly, we can refrain from buying the newer glass. Barring that, we who know the reproductions can label them as such when the opportunity arises.

"ADAM"

Privately produced out of Korea through St. Louis Importing Company

The new Adam butter is still being offered at $7.00 wholesale. Identification of the new is easy. The following only applies to butter dishes and cannot be used to determine authenticity of other items in this pattern.

Top: Notice the veins in the leaves.
New: Large leaf veins do not join or touch in center of leaf.
Old: Large leaf veins all touch or join center vein on the old.

A further note in the original Adam butter dish – the veins of all the leaves at the center of the design are very clear-cut and precisely molded, whereas in the new, these center leaf veins are very indistinct and almost invisible in open leaf of the center design.

Bottom: Place butter dish bottom upside down for observation.
New: Four "arrowhead-like" points line up in the northwest, northeast, southeast and southwest directions.
Old: Four "arrowhead-like" points line up in north, east, south and west directions.

There are very bad mold lines and very glossy light pink color on those new butter dishes I have examined, but these could be improved.

NEW "AVOCADO"

(pink, frosted pink, yellow, blue, red, amethyst, dark green, frost green)
INDIANA GLASS COMPANY, Tiara Exclusives Line, 1974...

Thus far, the company has only overlapped the original glass colors in pink. Green has been made, but note its a darker shade than the original green. A few additional items were made in yellow, but that was never a problem for collectors since yellow was not an original color. The original pink color is lighter in shade than this newer pink which has a slight orange tint.

Some of these sets, such as red, were made in limited editions as a selling point with buyers who are hopeful that someday they may be more valuable. Perhaps they shall; but I personally feel it will take many years for these to command more than their original value.

CHERRY BLOSSOM ⊂━━━━━━━━━━━━━━⊃
(pink, green, blue, delphite, red, cobalt blue, various iridized colors)
PRIVATELY PRODUCED IN 1973...

In 1973 the Depression glass world was stunned with the appearance of a child's butter dish and some odd-looking child's cups – odd because no child's butter dish was made originally and because in the bottoms of the cups, the cherry design was hanging upside-down. Since then, the upside-down design has been rectified and some saucers and plates have appeared. However, all these reproductions are easily spotted. **The child's creamer and sugar have not been reproduced!**

In 1977 butter dishes and shakers appeared. Some shakers in pink and green were dated '77; other pink, green, and delphite shakers appeared non-dated. These shakers are readily recognizable by the almost squared protrusions around the top edge of the shakers. I call them helicopter blades. On the original shakers these protrusions are more rounded and they extend only slightly outward from the top. If you wish to carry your examinations further than that, the design on the shakers is weaker in spots on the newer versions. Only two original pairs of pink shakers have ever been found!

The butter dishes pose a bit more problem in distinguishing old from new except in the pretty blue color which wasn't an original color. However, if you use your tactile sense and feel the design inside the butter top, you will find it very sharply defined in the new; the knob on the new top is also very sharply defined whereas in the old, the knob is more smoothly formed.

Again, about ½" from the edge of the new top, you will notice one ring or band. In the old, there are two distinct indented rings or bands to be noted there. Unfortunately, there are several generations of these repros.

CHERRY BLOSSOM

I could write a book on the differences between old and new scalloped bottom, AOP Cherry pitchers. The easiest way to tell the differences is to turn the pitcher over. My old Cherry pitcher has nine cherries on the bottom. (This is not true for all pitchers!) The new one only has seven. Further, the branch crossing the bottom of my old Cherry pitcher LOOKS like a branch. It's knobby and gnarled and has several leaves and cherry stems directly attached to it. The new pitcher just has a bald strip of glass halving the bottom of the pitcher. Further, the old cherry pitchers have a plain glass background for the cherries and leaves in the bottom of the pitcher. In the new pitchers, there's a rough, filled-in, straw-like background. You see no plain glass (My reproduction Cherry pitcher cracked sitting in a box by my typing stand – another tendency which I understand is common to the new!)

As for the new tumblers, the easiest way to tell old from the new is to look at the ring dividing the patterned portion of the glass from the plain glass lip. The old tumblers have three indented rings dividing the pattern from the plain glass rim. The new has only one. Further, as in the pitcher, the arching encircling the cherry blossoms on the new tumblers is very sharply ridged. On the old tumblers, that arching is so smooth you can barely feel it. Again, the pattern at the bottom of the new tumblers is brief and practically nonexistent in the center curve of the glass bottom. This was sharply defined on most of the old tumblers. The pattern, what there is, on the new tumblers mostly hugs the center of the foot.

Several different people have gotten into the act of making reproduction Cherry Blossom. We've even enjoyed some reproductions of reproduc-

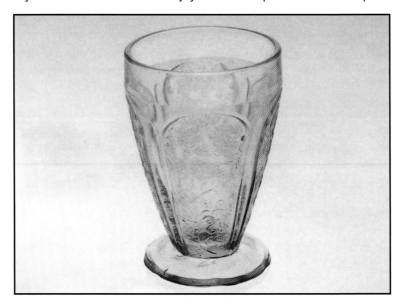

CHERRY BLOSSOM ⊂══════════════════⊃

tions! All the items pictured on the next pages are extremely easy to spot as reproductions once you know what to look for with the possible exception of the 13" divided platter pictured at the back. It's too heavy, weighing 2¾ pounds and has a thick, ⅜" of glass in the bottom; but the design isn't too bad! The edges of the leaves aren't smooth; but neither are they serrated like old leaves. As with old glass, these new pieces vary over the years; so remember, it is BUYER BEWARE!

Now for a quick run-down of the various items.

The Cherry child's dishes were first made in 1973. First to appear was a child's cherry cup with a slightly lop-sided handle and having the cherries hanging upside-down when the cup was held in the right hand. (This defiance of gravity was due to the inversion of the design when the mold, taken from an original cup, was inverted to create the outside of the "new" cup.) After I reported this error, it was quickly corrected by re-inverting the inverted mold. These later cups were thus improved in design but slightly off color. The saucers tended to have slightly off-center designs, too. Next came the "child's butter dish" which was never made by Jeannette. It was essentially the child's cup, without a handle, turned upside-down over the saucer and having a little blob of glass added as a knob for lifting purposes. You could get this item in pink, green, light blue, cobalt, gray-green and iridescent carnival colors.

Two-Handled Tray - Old: 1⅞ lbs; ³⁄₁₈" glass in bottom; leaves and cherries east/west from north/south handles; leaves have real spine and serrated edges; cherry stems end in triangle of glass.

Two-Handled Tray - New: 2⅛ lbs; ¼" glass in bottom; leaves and cherries north/south with the handles; canal-type leaves (but uneven edges); cherry stem ends before cup-shaped line.

Cake Plate - New: Color too light pink, leaves have too many parallel veins which give them a "feathery" look; arches at plate edge don't line up with lines on inside of the rim to which the feet are attached.

8½" Bowl - New: Crude leaves with smooth edges; veins in parallel lines.

Cereal Bowl - New: Wrong shape, looks like 8½" bowl, 2" center.

Cereal Bowl - Old: Large center, 2½" inside ring, nearly 3½" if you count the outer rim before the sides turn up.

Plate - New: Center has smooth edged leaves, fish spine type center leaf portion; weighs one pound plus; feels thicker at edge with mold offset lines clearly visible on edge.

Plate - Old: Center leaves look like real leaves with spines, veins, and serrated edges; weighs ¾ pound; clean edges; no mold offset on edge.

Cup - New: Area in bottom left free of design; canal leaves; smooth, thick top to cup handle (old has triangle grasp point).

Saucer - New: Off-set mold line edge; canal leaf center.

NEW FLORAL
IMPORTING COMPANY OUT OF GEORGIA

The big news in Floral is that reproduction shakers are now being found in pink, red, cobalt blue and a dark green color. Cobalt blue, red, and the dark green Floral shakers are of little concern since they were never made in these colors originally. The green is darker than the original green but not as deep as Forest green. The pink shakers are not only a very good pink, but they are also a very good copy. There are lots of minor variations in design and leaf detail to someone who knows glassware well, but I have always tried to pick out a point that anyone can use to determine validity whether he be a novice or professional. There is one easy way to tell the Floral reproductions. Take off the top and look at the threads where the lid screws onto the shaker. On the old there are a PAIR of parallel threads on each side or at least a pair on one side which end right before the mold seams down each side. The new Floral has one continuous line thread which starts on one side and continues around the shaker until it ends above the beginning line on the other side. There is approximately one inch of overlapped thread making two lines for that inch; but the whole thread is one continuous line and not two separate ones as on the old. No other Floral reproductions have been made as of May 1998.

NEW "FLORENTINE NO. 1"
IMPORTING COMPANY OUT OF GEORGIA

Although a picture of a reproduction shaker is not shown, I would like for you to know of its existence.

Florentine No. 1 shakers have been reproduced in pink, red, and cobalt blue. There may be other colors to follow. I only have one reproduction sample, and it is difficult to know if all shakers will be as badly molded as this one. I can say by looking at this one shaker that there is little or no design on the bottom. No red or cobalt blue Florentine No. 1 shakers have ever been found; so, those are no problem. The pink is more difficult. I am comparing this one to several old pairs from my shop. The old shakers have a major open flower on each side. There is a top circle on this blossom with three smaller circles down each side. The seven circles form the outside of the blossom. The new blossom looks more like a strawberry with no circles forming the outside of the blossom. This repro blossom looks like a poor drawing! Do not use the Floral thread test for the Florentine No. 1 shakers, however. It won't work for Florentine although these are made by the same importing company out of Georgia.

NEW "FLORENTINE NO. 2"

A reproduced footed Florentine No. 2 pitcher and footed juice tumbler appeared last year. First to surface was a cobalt blue set that alerted knowledgeable collectors that something was amiss. Next, sets of red, dark green and two shades of pink began to be seen at the local flea markets. All these colors were dead giveaways as the footed pitcher was never made in any of these shades or hues.

The new pitchers are approximately ¼" shorter than the original and have a flatter foot as opposed to the domed foot of the old. The mould line on the lip of the newer pitcher extends ½" below the lip while only ⅜" below on the original. All of the measurements could vary over time with the reproductions and may even vary on the older ones. The easiest way to tell the old from the new, besides the colors, is by the handles. The new handles are ⅞" wide, but the older ones were only ¾" wide. That ⅛" seems even bigger than that when you sit them side by side.

The juice tumbler is not as apparent as the pitcher, but there are two major discrepancies as I examine them. The old juice stands 4" tall and the diameter of the base is 2⅛". The reproduction is shorter and smaller in base diameter. It is only 3¹⁵⁄₁₈" tall and 2" in diameter. These are small differences, I know, but color is the most significant difference!

Iris 6½" footed ice tea tumblers (new on left).

Iris dinner plate (new on left).

New Iris

New tumblers have two distinct differences. First, turn these upside down and feel the rays on the foot. New rays are very sharp and will almost hurt your finger if you press on them hard. Old tumbler rays are rounded and feel smooth in comparison. The paneled design on the new tumbler gets very weak in several places as you rotate it in you hand. Old tumbler paneled designs stay bold around the entire tumbler.

New dinner plates have two characteristics readily discerned from the old. The extreme edge of the pattern on the new dinners is pointed outward (upside down V). Old dinner plate designs usually end looking like a stack of the letter V, though optical illusions sometimes distort that a bit. Also, the inside rim of the new dinners slopes inward toward the center of the plate, whereas original inside rims are almost perpendicular and steeper.

NEW "MADRID"
(amber, pink, crystal, blue, teal)
FEDERAL GLASS COMPANY, 1976 – 1977, 1980s, 1990s

New Madrid was introduced by Federal as "Recollection" in 1976 ostensibly for the Bicentennial. Each piece was dated '76 as shown here on a plate edge. The color was a deeper amber than the old.

The butter dish knob has mold marks running from north to south on the new; the mold marks run east to west on the old. I mention this only because on occasion new tops are "married" to old bottoms in an attempt to do a bit of "wool pulling."

Other items introduced in 1977 were candleholders, creamer and sugar with no lid, a footed candy and cover, a footed square bowl and a footed cake plate. These last three footed pieces were not duplicates of the original Madrid. However, due to the first issues not selling so well, many stores failed to stock these latter pieces.

NEW "MADRID"

Indiana Glass issued "Recollection" glass in colors made originally. Instead of creating new collectibles in colors never made, they wiped out many a collector's dreams of financial profit by remaking glassware long discontinued. Shown above is the "new" Recollection Pink Madrid. Thankfully, not much pink was made in the 1930s when Federal made Madrid. The picture at the top shows new concepts in design that were never made. There are other pedestal pieces using the candlestick for the base besides the cake plate shown. Once you have seen the pale, washed-out pink on any of these items, you will never have trouble spotting these culprits.

Blue has been made in all of the pieces shown in pink. It is a vivid blue when compared to the older, subtle "Madonna Blue" shade made by Federal originally. The newest color is teal, which is a very greenish shade of blue.

NEW "MAYFAIR"

(pink, green, blue, cobalt [shot glasses], 1977 onward; pink, green, "brownish" amethyst, cobalt blue, red [cookie jars], 1982; pink, red, cobalt blue [shakers], 1988; pink, cobalt blue [juice pitchers], 1993...)

Mayfair cookie jars, at cursory glance, have a base which has a very indistinct design. It will feel smooth to the touch, it's so faint. In the old cookie jars, there's a distinct pattern which feels like raised embossing to the touch. Next, turn the bottom upside-down. The new bottom is perfectly smooth. The old bottom contains a 1¾" mold circle rim that is raised enough to catch your fingernail in it. There are other distinctions as well; but that is the quickest way to tell old from new.

In the Mayfair cookie lid, the new design (parallel to the straight side of the lid) at the edge curves gracefully toward the center "V" shape (rather like bird wings in flight); in the old, that edge is flat, a straight line going into the "V" (like airplane wings sticking straight out from the side of the plane as you face it head-on.)

The green color of the cookie jar, as you can see from the picture, is not the pretty, yellow/green color of true green Mayfair. It also doesn't "glow" under black light as the old green does.

The shot glass (which is hard to find in the original) has also been made in this pattern. The green (totally wrong shade) and blue are no problem since the shot glasses have never been found in these colors originally. The difficulty comes with the pink.

Generally speaking, the newer shot glass has a heavier overall look. The bottom area tends to have a thicker rim of glass. Often, the "pink" coloring isn't right; it may be too light, it may be too orange. However, if these cursory examinations fail, there are other points to check.

First, notice the stem of the flower. You have a single stem in the new flower. At the base of the stem in the old glass, the stem separates into an "A" shape. Further, look at the leaves on the stem. In the new design, the leaf itself is hollow with the veins molded in. In the old glass, the leaf portion is molded in and the veining is left hollow. In the center of the flower, the dots (anther) cluster entirely to one side of the old design and are rather distinct. Nothing like that occurs in the newer version.

The juice pitchers shown below are photographed to show the bottoms. Note the original blue has a distinct mold circle which is missing on all reproduction pitchers. This and the oddly applied handles on the repros make these easily spotted!

Repro Mayfair Shaker

	Old	New
Diameter of opening	¾"	⅝"
* Diameter of lid	⅞"	¾"
Height	4¹/₁₈"	4"
Corner Ridges on Shaker	Rise ½ way to top then smooth out	Rise to top and are quite pronounced

* Most immediately noticeable factor.

NEW "MISS AMERICA"

(crystal, green, pink, ice blue, red amberina)
PRIVATELY PRODUCED 1977...

The new butter dish in "Miss America" design is probably the best of the newer products; yet there are three distinct differences to be found between the original butter top and the newly-made one. Since the value of the butter dish lies in the top, it seems more profitable to examine it.

In the new butter dishes pictured, notice that the panels reaching the edge of the butter bottom tend to have a pronounced curving, skirt-like edge. In the original dish, there is much less curving at the edge of these panels.

Second, pick up the top of the new dish and feel up inside it. If the butter top knob is filled with glass so that it is convex (curved outward), the dish is new; the old knob area is concave (curved inward).

Finally, from the underside, look through the top toward the knob. In the original butter dish you would see a perfectly-formed multi-sided star; in the newer version, you see distorted rays with no visible points.

Shakers have been made in green, pink and crystal. The shakers will have new tops; but since some old shakers have been given new tops, that isn't conclusive at all. Unscrew the lid. Old shakers have a very neatly formed ridge of glass on which to screw the lid. It overlaps a little and has neatly rounded off ends. Old shakers stand 3⅜" tall without the lid. Most new ones stand 3¼" tall. Old shakers have almost a forefinger's depth inside (female finger) or a fraction shy of 2½". These vary as there are reproductions of the reproductions! Most new shakers have an inside depth of 2", about the second digit bend of a female's finger. (I'm doing finger depths since most of you will have those with you at the flea market, rather than a tape measure.) In men, the old shaker's depth covers my knuckle; the new shaker leaves my knuckle exposed. Most new shakers simply have more glass on the inside of the shaker – something you can spot from 12 feet away. The hobs are more rounded on most newer shakers, particularly near the stem and seams; in the old shaker these areas remained pointedly sharp!

New Miss America tumblers have ½" of glass in the bottom, have a smooth edge on the bottom of the glass with no mold rim and show only two distinct mold marks on the sides of the glass. Old tumblers have only ¼" of glass in the bottom, have a distinct mold line rimming the bottom of the tumbler and have four distinct mold marks up the sides of the tumbler. The new green tumbler doesn't "glow" under black light as did the old.

New Miss America pitchers are all perfectly smooth rimmed at the top edge above the handle. All old pitchers that I have seen have a "hump" in the top rim of the glass above the handle area, rather like a camel's hump. The very bottom diamonds next to the foot in the new pitchers "squash" into elongated diamonds. In the old pitchers, these get noticeably smaller, but they retain their diamond shape. Only the non-ice lip pitcher has been reproduced!

NEW "ROYAL LACE"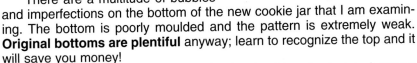
(cobalt blue)
Importing Company from Taiwan

The first thing you notice about the reproduced pieces is the extra dark, vivid cobalt blue color! It is not the soft cobalt blue originally made by Hazel Atlas. So far, only the cookie jar, juice and water tumblers have been made as of May 2000.

The original cookie jar lid has a mould seam that bisects the center of the pattern on one side, and runs across the knob and bisects the pattern on the opposite side. There is no mould line at all on the reproduction.

There are a multitude of bubbles and imperfections on the bottom of the new cookie jar that I am examining. The bottom is poorly moulded and the pattern is extremely weak. **Original bottoms are plentiful** anyway; learn to recognize the top and it will save you money!

As for tumblers, the first reproduction tumblers had plain bottoms without the four pointed design which makes these simple to distinguish. The new juice tumbler has a bottom design, but it is as large as the one on the water tumbler and covers the entire bottom of the glass. Originally, this design was very small and did not encompass the whole bottom as does this reproduction. Additionally, there are design flaws on both size tumblers that stand out. The four ribs between each of the four designs on the side of the repro tumblers protrude far enough to catch your fingernail. The original tumblers have a very smooth, flowing design that you can only feel. The other distinct flaw is a semi-circular design on the rim of the glass above those four ribs. Originally these were very tiny on both tumblers with five oval leaves in each. There are three complete

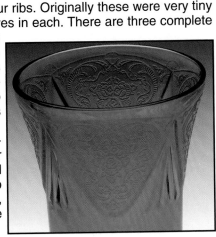

diamond-shaped designs in the new tumblers with two being doubled diamonds (diamond shapes within diamonds); and the semi-circular design almost touches the top rim! There's at least an ⅛" of glass above the older "fan."

Also, on the bottom of the tumblers, the four flower petal center designs in the old is open-ended leaving ⅛" of open glass at the tip of each petal. In the new version, these ends are closed, causing the petals to be pointed on the end.

NEW "SANDWICH"
(crystal)
ANCHOR HOCKING GLASS COMPANY

At present, only the cookie jar has been re-introduced to use the jargon of today. The newer jar is much larger when compared with the old. To date, no other pieces have been made (May, 2000)!

	New	Old
Height	10¼"	9¼"
Opening Width	5½"	4⅞"
Diameter/Largest Part	22"	19"

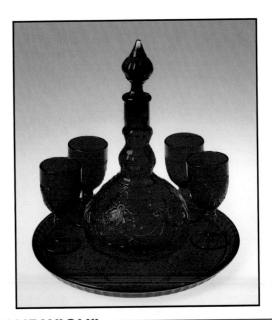

NEW "SANDWICH"
(amber, blue, red, green)
INDIANA GLASS COMPANY, Tiara Exclusive Line 1969 . . .

In recent years, Indiana Sandwich in amber, the smokey blue, green, and a sprayed red over crystal have been issued. In 1969 came red in quite a few pieces and these are difficult to tell from the older pieces of the 1930s. Any piece you see in amber or blue is of recent origin.

Bad news for collectors came in 1978 when Tiara announced that they were going to issue the Sandwich in crystal from decanter sets down to the domed butter dish. My advice here is to be wary of paying any high prices for the old at this time. Since many of the original molds are being used, there is little difference.

Green is now being made but it is a pale, washed-out green and will not glow under a black light as does the original green. Pictured at the top is the red decanter set and at the bottom is the teal butter dish which was a Tiara premium of the early 1980s. The wines shown in red are the earlier style. Those made in green and later in amber are shaped more like Iris cocktails.

NEW "SHARON"

(blue, dark green, light green, pink, burnt umber, red, cobalt blue)
PRIVATELY PRODUCED 1976 . . .

A blue Sharon butter turned up in 1976 and created a sensation. The blue was the color of Mayfair blue; but this color was unknown in the Sharon pattern. This fluke helped to quickly inform Depression enthusiasts that new editions were being made available.

In similar colors, you can distinguish between the old and the new butter dishes by noticing that the bottom ridge of the newer butter dish is sharply defined; the old bottom ledge is barely defined. Also, the top of the newer butter dish is heavier and thicker than the old – in most instances, it even weighs more. The knob is easier to grasp on the new butter dishes as it sticks up higher and you've more room to fit your finger around the knob and grasp the top. In the old butter dish tops, the knob fits so closely to the top that it makes it hard to grasp the knob.

In 1977 a "cheese dish" appeared having the same top as the butter. I put the name in quotes because it is but a parody of the original cheese dish. The new bottom of the dish is about half-way between a flat plate and butter dish bottom and is over thick, giving it an awkward appearance. The real cheese dish bottom more nearly resembles a salad plate with a raised rim. These "cheese dishes" are easily spotted as being new.

The newest reproduction in Sharon is a too light pink creamer and sugar with lid. They are pictured with their "Made in Taiwan" label. These

NEW "SHARON"

sell for around $15.00 for the pair and are also easy to spot as reproductions. I'll just mention the most obvious differences. Turn the creamer so you are looking directly at the spout. In the old creamer the mold line runs dead center of that spout; in the new, the mold line runs decidedly to the left of center spout.

On the sugar, the leaves and roses are "off" but not enough to DESCRIBE it to new collectors. Therefore, look at the center design, both sides, at the stars located at the very bottom of the motif. A thin leaf stem should run directly from that center star upward on BOTH sides. In this new sugar, the stem only runs from one; it stops way short of the star on one side. OR look inside the sugar bowl at where the handle attaches to the bottom of the bowl. In the new bowl, this attachment looks like a perfect circle; in the old, its an upside-down "v"-shaped tear drop.

As for the sugar lid, the knob of the new lid is perfectly smooth as you grasp its edges. The old knob has a mold seam running mid circumference. You could tell these two lids apart blind-folded.

While there is a hair's difference between the height, mouth opening diameter, and inside depth of the old Sharon shakers and those newly produced, I won't attempt to upset you with those 16th and 32nd of a degree of difference. Suffice it to say that in physical shape, they are very close. However, as concern design, they're miles apart. The old shakers have true-appearing roses. The flowers really LOOK like roses. On the new shakers, they look like poorly drawn circles with wobbly concentric rings. The leaves are not as clearly defined on the new shakers as the old. However, forgetting all that, in the old shakers, the first design you see below the lid is a ROSE BUD. It's angled like a rocket shooting off into outer space with three leaves at the base of the bud (where the rocket fuel would burn out). In the new shakers, this "bud" has become four paddles of a windmill. It's the difference between this and this .

The shakers wholesale for around $6.50 a pair.

A Sharon candy dish has been made by the infamous St. Louis group. It is very crude, thick and should pose no problems. Be aware that it does exist and know your dealer.

Glossary

Amber - brownish yellow color (see Madrid or Patrician photo for example).

Amethyst - a light, pastel purple as opposed to black amethyst which appears black until held to strong light whereby it shows deep purple.

Apricot - a dark yellow color, yet lighter in shade than amber; usually used to describe the darkest shade of Princess than topaz.

AOP - abbreviation for "all over pattern," usually used to describe Cherry Blossom.

Berry Bowl - term used by many glass companies to describe a round bowl.

Bonbon - a candy dish, usually uncovered.

Bread and Butter Plate - usually a 6" plate in a pattern that does not have a sherbet.

Cake Plate - a heavy, flat plate, usually having three legs.

Carnival - older, iridized glassware from early 1900s; also term used to describe the color of Floragold or an iridized pattern.

Celery - usually a long, narrow, flat dish; in Colonial, a two-handled dish taller than the sugar.

Cheese Dish - a covered dish, the bottom of which is normally flatter than that of the butter dish.

Chigger Bite - a term auctioneers use to describe a small chip on a dish.

Chop Plate - a large, flat plate called a salver by some companies.

Chunked - a polite way to describe a badly damaged piece of glass.

Claret - tall goblet of varying size depending upon company terminology.

Closed Handled - having solid tab handles.

Coaster - glass liner sometimes doubling as an ashtray.

Cobalt Blue - a deep, dark blue color (shown in Moderntone or Moondrops).

Comport/Compote - term used to denote small, open candy dish which is stemmed.

Concentric Rings - circles within circles; gradually increasing or decreasing sized circles.

Console Bowl - centerpiece bowl, usually with candlesticks.

Cordial - small goblet of varying size depending upon company terminology.

Cracker Jar - term for what would a modern-day cookie jar; they were sold with certain brands of products packed inside them.

Cream Soup - a two-handled bouillon or consomme dish.

Decanter - usually a stoppered bottle for wine.

Delphite - a light blue opaque color; sometimes referred to as "blue milk glass."

Demitasse - a smaller than normal cup with saucer.

Domino Tray - a tray with a ring for creamer to reside in; the remaining surface within the tray being meant to hold sugar cubes.

Ebony - black color.

Etched - design cut into glass; usually found on better quality glass.

Fired-On - color applied and baked on at the factory.

Flashed-On - color added over crystal; usually wears off as opposed to the fired-on color which does not wear off with use.

Flat - a non-footed dish; dish without a footed base or stem.

Fluted - scalloped edge.

Frog - heavy glass holed flower stem holder.

Goblet - a stemmed, bowl-shaped tumbler.

Gravy Boat - oval-shaped bowl used for serving gravy; often with a type of spout.

Grill Plate - a usually tri-sectioned plate of the type used in restaurants to keep the meat and vegetables divided from each other.

Hat Shaped - bowl looking like an up-turned hat.

Glossary

Hot Plate - glass plate used for setting hot items on the table as a protection for the table or table spread.

Ice Blue - very light, crystal blue color.

Ice Bucket - a milk bucket-like container for holding ice cubes.

Ice Lip - a guard or fold molded about the lip of a pitcher to keep ice from falling out into the glass when pouring from the pitcher.

Jadite - an opaque, light green color.

Jam Jar - small, covered jar for holding jam or preserves.

Luncheon Plate - usually an 8" or 9" plate, smaller than a dinner plate.

Mayonnaise - an open, cone-shaped compote or flat bowl with underliner.

Milk Glass - a white glassware, the color of milk, usually heavy.

Mold/Mould - a usually two-part encasement into which hot glass is poured and a glass object is formed; depression glass was primarily glassware made from molds rather than being blown or formed by hand.

Monax - white color produced by MacBeth Evans, usually very thin.

Motif - the pattern or design on glass.

Mug - a heavy cup, usually flat bottomed.

Nappy - old word denoting a bowl.

Opalescent - white rimmed flowing into color.

Open Handled - handles having an opening for the finger or hand to reach through.

Parfait - a tall, ice cream dish of the type used for sundaes in soda fountains.

Pickle Dish - an oblong dish used for serving pickles; smaller than a celery.

Platinum Band - an applied silver colored rim on glassware.

Platonite - Hazel Atlas heat-resistant white glass often colored by a fired-on process.

Platter - oblong or oval-shaped meat dish.

Preserve Dish - tall, footed dish often used as a candy.

Rayed - arrows or spoke-like designs on glass bottoms.

Relish - oblong dish, sometimes referred to as a pickle dish.

Rolled Edge - glassware having an edge curved in toward or out away from center.

Rope Edge - glassware with an edge having a rope-like design embedded in it.

Rose Bowl - small, curved-in edged bowl, usually having a small center hole and usually tri-footed.

Salad Plate - usually 7"-7½" plate, for serving salads.

Salver - large, 11"-12" non-handled serving plate.

Sandwich Server - a salver or sometimes a handled, often center-handled, serving plate.

SASE - short for self-addressed, stamped envelope.

Sherbet - small, usually footed, ice cream or dessert dish.

Teal - a blue-green color by all companies except Jeannette.

Tidbit - a two- or three-tiered serving dish made of increasingly smaller plates connected by a center metal pole, around 12"-15" tall.

Topaz - bright yellow colored glassware.

Trivet - a three-footed hot plate, usually about 7" in diameter, similar in design to three-footed cake plates but much smaller in diameter.

Tumbler - a glass.

Tumble-Up - a glass bottle with long neck having a small tumbler seated upside-down over the bottle neck serving as the bottle top; usually used on nightstand by bed.

Ultra-Marine - Jeannette's blue-green color.

Vaseline - a glowing yellow colored glassware similar to the color of the jell-like substance of the same name.

A publication I recommend:

DEPRESSION GLASS DAZE
THE ORIGINAL NATIONAL DEPRESSION GLASS NEWSPAPER

Depression Glass Daze, the Original, National monthly newspaper dedicated to the buying, selling and collecting of colored glassware of the 20's and 30's. We average 48 pages. Each issue is filled with feature articles by top-notch columnists, reader "finds," club happenings, show news, a china corner, a current listing of new glass issues to beware of and a multitude of ads!! You can find it in the DAZE! Keep up with what's happening in the dee gee world with a subscription to the DAZE. Buy, sell or trade from the convenience of your easy chair. **One Year Subscription - $21.00.**

Name _____

Address_____

City_____ State_____ Zip_____

Foreign subscribers - please add $1.00 per year

☐ Check Enclosed ☐ Please Bill Me ☐ MasterCard ☐ Visa

Card Number_____ Exp. Date_____

Signature_____

Send to: D.G.D., Box 57GF, Otisville, MI 48463
(Please allow 30 days.)

A website I recommend:
http://www.glassshow.com

Additional Books by Gene Florence

Collectible Glassware from the 40s, 50s & 60s	$19.95
Collector's Encyclopedia of Depression Glass	$19.95
Collector's Encyclopedia of Occupied Japan 1st, 2nd, 5th series	$14.95
Elegant Glassware of the Depression Era	$19.95
Kitchen Glassware of the Depression Years	$19.95
Very Rare Glassware of the Depression Years, Third Series	$24.95
Very Rare Glassware of the Depression Years, Fifth Series	$24.95
Very Rare Glassware of the Depression Years, Sixth Series	$24.95
Florence's Glassware Pattern Identification Guide, Volume 1	$18.95
Florence's Glassware Pattern Identification Guide, Volume 2	$19.95
Pocket Guide to Depression Glass	$9.95
Glass Candlesticks of the Depression Era	$24.95
Stemware Identification	$24.95
Anchor Hocking's Fire-King & More	$24.95

Add $3.00 postage for first book and 40 cents for each additional book.

Copies of these books may be ordered from:

Gene Florence – P.O. Box 22186, Lexington, KY 40522
or
Collector Books – P.O. Box 3009, Paducah, KY 42003-3009